INSIGHT GUIDES

WASHINGTON, DC
POCKET GUIDE

www.insightguides.com/USA

⊙ Walking Eye App

Your Insight Pocket Guide purchase includes a free download of the destination's corresponding eBook. It is available now from the free Walking Eye container app in the App Store and Google Play. Simply download the Walking Eye container app to access the eBook dedicated to your purchased book. The app also features free information on local events taking place and activities you can enjoy during your stay, with the option to book them. In addition, premium content for a wide range of other destinations is available to purchase in-app.

HOW TO DOWNLOAD THE WALKING EYE APP

Available on purchase of this guide only.

1. Visit our website: www.insightguides.com/walkingeye
2. Download the Walking Eye container app to your smartphone (this will give you access to your free eBook and the ability to purchase other products)
3. Select the scanning module in the Walking Eye container app
4. Scan the QR Code on this page – you will be asked to enter a verification word from the book as proof of purchase
5. Download your free eBook* for travel information on the go

* Other destination apps and eBooks are available for purchase separately or are free with the purchase of the Insight Guide book

TOP 10 ATTRACTIONS

WHITE HOUSE
Home to the President of the United States. See page 23.

THE UNITED STATES CAPITOL
The seat of the U.S. Congress. See page 35.

THE NATIONAL GALLERY OF ART
An excellent showcase for Western art from the Middle Ages to the present. See page 68.

THE WASHINGTON CATHEDRAL
The sixth largest cathedral on earth, built in Neo Gothic style. See page 58.

THE WASHINGTON MONUMENT
This white obelisk is a tribute to George Washington. See page 31.

THE NATIONAL MUSEUM OF AMERICAN HISTORY
A fun and fascinating collection. See page 64.

THE ZOO
One of the oldest zoos in the United States. See page 57.

ARLINGTON NATIONAL CEMETERY
The nation's war heroes have been laid to rest here. See page 76.

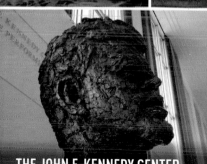

THE JOHN F. KENNEDY CENTER
See a theater, dance or music performance at this modern center. See page 79.

MOUNT VERNON
The plantation house of George Washington on the banks of the Potomac River. See page 84.

A PERFECT DAY

9.00am

Breakfast
Enjoy an artisanal toast and crafted coffee at Slipstream (see page 108) or simply grab delicious coffee to go at Peregrine Espresso.

12 noon

Holocaust museum
In this unusual museum you'll step into another era, paying homage to the victims of the Holocaust. Then, as it's already past lunchtime, stop for lunch at a local cafe.

9.30am

First things first
Take a walk to the White House (advance reservations only – see online) to admire the magnificent state rooms and take photos. If you are not lucky enough to have a tour of the house, take a walk in the President's Park and view it from the outside.

11.30am

Washington Monument
Cross Constitution Avenue and look up at the towering Washington Monument which at its 554 ft (169 meters) is the world's tallest stone structure. Then walk to the United States Holocaust Memorial Museum at Wallenberg Place.

2.00pm

The Mall
Stroll down the green Mall for 1.2 miles (1.8km), visiting some of the city's best museums along the way, including the National Museum of Natural History, the National Museum of American History and the National Gallery of Art.

10.00pm

On the town

Hit the 9:30 Club (815 V St. NW), arguably the best live music venue in Washington. Alternatively, buy tickets for one of the shows at the John F. Kennedy Center for the Performing Arts.

5.30pm

Best buys

Enjoy your shopping spree and then settle down to relaxed dinner at one of restaurants at Union Station's Food Mall. Then as night begins to fall, take a cab (15 minutes' drive) over to the Lincoln Memorial.

4.30pm

Capitol Hill

Walk to Capitol Hill to see the impressive seat of Congress with spectacular views of the entire Mall. For a break from sightseeing, take the metro to Union Station where retail stores abound.

9.00pm

City of light

At night, the grandly illuminated Lincoln Memorial is a sight to behold, as are the Jefferson and Roosevelt Memorials standing tall over the Tidal Basin nearby.

CONTENTS

INTRODUCTION

Washington DC, although not one of the 50 United States, is truly the all-American city. In the best sense of the word, the nation's capital belongs to the people, who look upon it as half-shrine, half fun-fair, and as such it has long been one of the most popular family vacation spots in the country. No visitor should miss this uniquely American experience.

In climate and flavor Washington is Southern, for it lies south of the Mason-Dixon Line, the boundary between Pennsylvania and Maryland that had traditionally separated the North from "Dixie," the South. It was the first modern city built from scratch to be a national capital. In 1790 George Washington himself picked the spot for the "Federal City" that was to bear his name, and laid the cornerstone of the Capitol; but he died before Congress first met here, in 1800. Virginia and Maryland ceded parts of their state territory along the Potomac River for the site set aside as the District of Columbia – "DC."

Broad avenues radiating like spokes from the Capitol and White House are lined with government buildings designed to impress. The architectural styles adopted over two centuries are a mirror of changing official taste, from Greek and Roman to contemporary steel and glass. There are no skyscrapers or industrial installations and there are plenty of open green spaces, parks, fountains, and monuments. If all this seems reminiscent of Paris, there is good reason. The man who laid out the plans for DC was Pierre Charles L'Enfant, a Frenchman inspired by memories of home.

Stark Memorials

The Vietnam Veterans Memorial's wall covered with the names of the dead makes no pretense of glorifying their sacrifice. Many visitors have tears in their eyes here, as they may also at President Kennedy's tombstone on the hillside overlooking Arlington National Cemetery's acres of graves.

Jefferson Memorial

Some of the monuments are both beautiful and central to American history. Preeminent is the Lincoln Memorial; the great seated statue of Abraham Lincoln, surrounded by the words of the Gettysburg Address, which many American schoolchildren learn by heart, symbolizes the healed trauma of the Civil War. It faces the spot where Martin Luther King, Jr. made his "I Have a Dream" address to civil rights marchers demanding fulfillment of Lincoln's ideals. Beyond the memorial's Reflecting Pool, the Washington Monument spears the clouds through a ring of flags. Nearby, cherry blossom trees that were a gift from Japan encircle the Potomac's Tidal Basin and the classic white marble temple dedicated to Thomas Jefferson, author of the Declaration of Independence.

Washington manages to combine the educational with the entertaining. Families with kids in tow line up to see Ford's Theatre, where Lincoln was assassinated; the dinosaurs at the Natural History Museum; George Washington's wooden false teeth at Mt. Vernon; and the famous panda bears at the National

Zoo. More lines form at the Air and Space Museum's exciting displays. Other offshoots of the Smithsonian Institution house a treasure trove of milestones gleaned from what could be called the American century.

Visitors fill the magnificent National Gallery of Art; they line up to see the original Shakespeare folios in the Folger Shakespeare Library, the Declaration of Independence at the National Archives, and the Gutenberg Bible at the Library of Congress; and they attend the concerts and stage productions at the Kennedy Center. They wander among the dogwood trees in the gardens of Dumbarton Oaks, stroll the tree-lined streets of Georgetown, and cluster in the Rotunda under the Capitol dome.

Most Washingtonians work for the government and are well-paid (with the highest federal payroll nationwide). They come from every state in the Union, are well educated, and there's a higher-than-average percentage of single women. For fun they go to the bars and restaurants of Adams Morgan and Georgetown. The latter, an elegant residential district founded in 1665 is noted for its shady streets lined with Georgian houses. Today, these are the homes of the capital's movers and shakers. Washington is also home to a number of leading colleges and universities, which add to the city's vibrant social scene.

In Washington, there's always something new or surprising going on. A person can stand for hours shouting protests in front of the FBI building and no one will bat an eye, while another camps 20 yards (18 m) from the White House to air a grievance. You'll see all types here: dawn commuter; parents on the school run; young executives; conventioneer with name badge; tourists; Georgetown dowager walking a pedigree dog; the after-work happy-hour gang and restaurant crowd, all forming a colorful tapestry. After a trip to DC, Americans return home feeling patriotic and edified. Foreign visitors leave with a sense of astonished discovery.

A BRIEF HISTORY

The idea of a purpose-built capital city is not so strange now. But it must have seemed wildly visionary in 1790 when Congress authorized the newly elected President Washington to select a site "not exceeding 10 miles square" on the Potomac River.

In the early years after American independence, Congress was more or less nomadic, convening in Philadelphia, Baltimore, Annapolis, New York, and several other cities. When a statue of George Washington was commissioned in 1783, Francis Hopkinson, one of the signatories of the Declaration of Independence, suggested that it be put on wheels so that it could follow Congress about. Philadelphia might well have become the legislators' permanent home but, in the same year, soldiers demanding back pay stormed a session of Congress there and the next meeting was prudently held in Princeton.

By this time, members from Southern states resented what they saw as excessive Northern influence; Northerners hated the prospect of a long journey to some Southern city. The North, however, had run up far greater debts in the independence struggle, so Thomas Jefferson, then Secretary of State, and Treasury Secretary Alexander Hamilton – rarely in accord – agreed to deliver the

George Washington

View of the "Federal City" in 1801

votes of their respective followers for a quid pro quo. If Congress were to take over the states' debts, the capital would be located as far south as the Potomac, with the exact place to be decided by George Washington himself.

CHOOSING THE SITE

Washington opted for the full 10 by 10 miles (16 by 16 km), in a diamond shape mostly on the Maryland bank but including some of the Virginia side of the river. (That piece went back to Virginia in 1846, destroying the symmetry.) Given the terms of the deal, it's clear why Washington chose this area. It included Alexandria, nearest town to his beloved estate of Mount Vernon; it incorporated Georgetown, at the furthest point that seagoing ships could reach on the Potomac. The new capital territory could have its own port, which was considered essential. There were already plans to cut a canal to bypass the river's rapids and offer a trade route with lands opening up to the west. Commissioners were appointed for this "Territory of Columbia" (the even less romantic word "District" crept in later), and it was they who simply announced the capital's name: the City of Washington.

THINKING BIG

The backdrop for the first president's inauguration in New York had been designed by a talented French engineer, Pierre Charles L'Enfant, a veteran of the Revolutionary War. Washington was obviously impressed, because he appointed the young officer to come up with a proposal for the layout of the new city. L'Enfant surveyed the unpromising terrain and produced a staggeringly ambitious scheme. Although a population of 8,000 was big in those days (only six cities in the new United States exceeded it), he dreamed of an eventual 800,000.

The Frenchman set to work in 1791–and ran straight into trouble. People were building wooden houses and huts where he demanded grand vistas. Bitter arguments blew up between the hot-tempered "L'Enfant Terrible" and those who thought free Americans ought to be able to build where they liked.

Only a year after he had begun, his disagreements with the commissioners had become so violent that the president felt compelled to dismiss him. It was a tragedy for the engineer and for the city, though mercifully many of the elements of L'Enfant's vision survived in the years that followed.

Work began on a mansion for the president, and Washington laid the cornerstone of the Capitol in 1793. Progress was slow, but by 1800 there were enough small offices for all 126 government officials to move from Philadelphia. The Congress was able to meet in the completed wing of the Capitol and

CITY DESIGNS

L'Enfant's plan used slight rises in the ground to settle the President's House and the Congress House at either end of a broad avenue, since named Pennsylvania. That didn't just make for a good view, it kept them out of the mud – a lot of this area was notoriously swampy. The two buildings would be the focal points for more avenues radiating from them. On a third low hill, where the present Washington Monument stands, there was to have been a statue of Washington on horseback. East and north of this basic triangle, the area would be filled in with a grid of streets.

John Adams could move into the White House for the end of his term as second president, although it was damp and far from finished, according to his wife Abigail. Others fared no better: the number of substantial houses in the city did not reach double figures.

In 1801, Jefferson became the first president to take the oath of office in Washington, in a ceremony deliberately devoid of ostentation. The new century generated new ambitions for the nation, but its capital was to be shamefully neglected. L'Enfant's "city of magnificent distances" was scorned as a "capital of miserable huts" and a "mud-hole" by members of the Congress. Carping voices never ceased suggesting that the capital should shift to somewhere else: fortunately, there was no consensus as to which place.

Plan of the city in 1818

THE BRITISH LIGHT A FIRE

War with Britain came again in 1812. In retaliation for American attacks on Canada, a British force under Admiral Cockburn landed in Maryland and occupied Washington. On August 24, 1814, the invaders set fire to the White House and other federal buildings, including the two completed wings of the Capitol. The buildings were gutted, but a torrent of rainfall that night luckily limited the damage

– but not before the White House had turned decidedly black.

Everyone had to find temporary accommodations, but at least indignation at the wicked British brought about a patriotic feeling for

Freedom to Slaves

In October 1859, the abolitionist John Brown raided Harpers Ferry, Virginia, calling on all slaves to revolt. He was hanged for treason, but hailed by many in the North as a martyr.

the capital. Agitation to find another site went out of fashion, though only the advent of railroads and the telegraph finally killed it off. Forty years of haphazard growth followed, with the addition of a few large buildings but scarcely any amenities.

CIVIL WAR CAPITAL

The 1850s saw the long-simmering pot of North-South division and resentment come to a boil. The South, fearing interference with the institution of slavery, insisted on states' rights vis à vis the Union. The North was determined to prevent slavery from spreading into new states that were forming in the territories of the west. Rancor in Congress turned from verbal to actual physical violence.

In the 1860 elections, the Democrats split between North and South and the pro-Union Republican candidate Abraham Lincoln was elected president entirely on votes from the Northern states. The South seceded and formed the Confederate States of America. All-out war ensued, and Washington, on the border between Union and Confederate forces, was the focus – both politically and geographically.

The Civil War was sparked when South Carolina troops fired on the federal base at Fort Sumter on April 12, 1861. Opposing armies were quickly formed around Washington and the Confederate capital of Richmond, Virginia, only about 100 miles (160 km) to the south. Most people thought it would soon be over, but the nightmare lasted four years. By the end, 600,000 had died in combat, either of wounds or from disease. Union forces tried to take Richmond several times, and Confederates tried twice to break into the North just inland from Washington, so some of the greatest battles took place around the city. At times even the Capitol was used as a hospital for the wounded. Government departments proliferated and more desks were squeezed in wherever they would fit.

The population of the capital doubled between 1861 and 1865, suddenly including 40,000 freed slaves. At last, the North's preponderance in population and industry began to prevail over the South's superior military leadership. The Southern hero, Robert E. Lee, his forces outnumbered and surrounded and with Richmond lost, surrendered to Ulysses S. Grant on April 9, 1865. Just five days later, Lincoln was assassinated at Ford's Theatre in Washington, while watching an English comedy with his wife, by a Confederate sympathizer.

In 1871, Ulysses S. Grant, then president, appointed a new city government for DC. Its administrator, Alexander "Boss" Shepherd, set about installing roads, street lights, and sewers and countless trees were planted. Civic and national pride in the city increased. People began to visit, to view the monuments and witness the documents that told the story of the birth of the United States.

L'Enfant Redeemed

Works were done more or less to L'Enfant's plan and as a result his reputation was redeemed. In 1909 he was reburied with honors in Arlington National Cemetery.

GROWTH, DEPRESSION, AND A NEW DEAL

World War I led to another huge increase in the bureaucracy. Temporary office buildings (that remained for decades) disfigured the Mall. Between the wars, foreign diplomats regarded Washington as a hardship post, a somnolent backwater lacking any finesse of culture or cuisine. The Depression that followed the Wall Street Crash of 1929 brought hunger marchers and a "Bonus Army" of war veterans to camp near the White House.

Franklin D. Roosevelt became president in 1933 with the promise of a New Deal to create employment by a huge program of public works. That, of course, meant many more jobs in the federal government, as well as for the lobbyists and lawyers that circle it like pilot fish around

Roosevelt signing the declaration of war against Japan

a whale. When 1941 brought the US into World War II, payrolls escalated once again and buildings went up with amazing speed. The world's largest office building, the Pentagon, took only 18 months to build and housed over 28,000 war planners.

TRANSFORMATION

Victory was followed by the Cold War and the McCarthy witch-hunts for real and imaginary communists. In 1954, the Supreme Court ruled against racial segregation in public (state) schools, and the capital was the first to comply. A plan mounted to build the Kennedy Center was meant to repair Washington's cultural deficiencies, though it would be many years before the complex was finished. The president it honored and his successor, Lyndon B. Johnson, campaigned for a better city.

Meanwhile, Martin Luther King, Jr. inspired the struggle of African Americans for the rights they had been promised a century before. His assassination in 1968 triggered the riots that ruined much of the old downtown area and set it back a decade.

The people of DC gradually gained – or regained – most of the democratic rights of "normal" US citizens over this period. They could at last vote in a presidential election, then for a Representative in Congress (though still not one with a full vote). In 1975, they could vote again for a city council and mayor. There is a movement afoot to make DC a state, so that it can also be represented in the Senate. The year 1976 saw celebrations for the bicentennial of the Declaration of Independence – and the opening of the first Metro line.

On September 11, 2001 terrorists hijacked American Airlines Flight 77 and deliberately crashed it into the Pentagon, killing 64 passengers and 125 people on the ground. After the attacks, security was increased exponentially with screening devices, metal detectors and vehicle barriers at many office and government buildings.

Barack Obama's Presidential Inauguration at the Capitol Building

Today Washington has a growing economy. It's the fourth largest metropolitan economy in the U.S. with a population of 659,000, of whom around 29 percent is employed by the federal government. As the country continues to battle economic recession, Washington remains almost immune.

HISTORICAL LANDMARKS

1600 Piscataway Native Americans live in the Washington DC area.

1791 George Washington picks a site for the new capital.

1800 The federal government officially moves to Washington

1802 Congress grants the city its first municipal charter.

1814 English troops burn some federal buildings in Washington.

1846 The Smithsonian Institute is established.

1862 Slavery is abolished in Washington DC.

1865 President Abraham Lincoln is assassinated at Ford's Theatre.

1888 Washington Monument opens.

1922 The Lincoln Memorial is dedicated.

1961 DC citizens get the right to vote in presidential elections.

1963 Over 200,000 people march on Washington and hear Martin Luther King's speech.

1972 The Watergate scandal.

1973 Residents get the right to vote for their mayor and city council.

1976 The Washington Metro opens.

1981 President Ronald Reagan is injured in an assassination attempt.

1992 The House of Representatives votes in favor of statehood for Washington DC but the Senate is against.

2001 A terrorist-hijacked plane crashes into the Pentagon, killing 64 passengers and 125 people on the ground.

2009 Barack Obama becomes the first African American President of the United States and moves into the White House (he is reelected in 2013).

2011 The White House and the Capitol are evacuated following a 5.8 multitude Virginia quake. The Washington Monument, the Smithsonian Castle and the Washington Cathedral suffer minor damage.

2013 Aaron Alexis shoots dead 12 and injures three people at the NAVSEA headquarters in Washington Navy Yard.

2015 Former Secretary of State Hillary Clinton formally enters the 2016 presidential race in a bid to become the first woman US president. The Supreme Court legalizes same-sex marriages in all 50 states.

WHERE TO GO

Fortunately, most of Washington's sights are concentrated in one part of the city. Practically all are in a rectangle extending from the Lincoln Memorial and the Watergate Complex in the west to the Library of Congress and Union Station in the east. Georgetown, northwest of this area, Dupont Circle, north of the White House, and Arlington, south across the Potomac, are easily accessible. Although the Metro system conveniently links most attractions, there is also the DC Circulator service operating on five Washington routes with buses arriving every 10 minutes and fares costing just $1 (see page 131).

THE WHITE HOUSE ❶

(1600 Pennsylvania Avenue, NW) No tour of Washington would be complete without a stop at the White House (www.nps.gov/whho), one of the most famous houses in history. Unfortunately, owing to security concerns, tours are limited to small groups of 10 or more. They can be arranged through local congressional representatives and for foreign nationals, through the respective embassies. Requests must be submitted at least 21 days in advance. Tours are free, self-guided and available Tue–Thur 7.30–11.30am and Fri–Sat 7.30am–1.30pm. Call the 24-hour information line at (202) 456-7041 for details. As an alternative to an official tour, be sure to spend time at the White House Visitor Center, at 1450 Pennsylvania Avenue, NW. The Center is open daily from 7.30am–4pm (tel: (202) 208-1631, 1-(800) 877-8339; www.nps.gov/whho; www.whitehouse.gov; closed Thanksgiving, Christmas and New Year's Day; free). It features exhibits on the history and architecture of the building, the furnishings, plus accounts of social events as well as the more mundane workings of daily life for the head of state, his family, and staff.

Lincoln Memorial, Washington Monument and the Capitol at dawn

President's Plants

Thomas Jefferson designed the White House gardens and planted dozens of sapling trees. Though none have survived, he is credited with fostering the tree-planting habit of successive presidents.

If the White House looks just right to us now, that may be because it is such a familiar image, an icon to represent the country. Pierre L'Enfant chose its site, at the other end of his broad avenue (now Pennsylvania) from the Capitol. The sweeping view L'Enfant envisaged between the two buildings was marred in 1836, when President Andrew Jackson sited the Treasury Building next door to the White House.

Thomas Jefferson suggested they hold a national competition to design the "President's House" (the actual name, the White House, already in use as a nickname before 1814, was not officially recognized by Congress till 1902) and put in an anonymous entry himself, which looked rather like his Monticello. It was beaten by a proposal from Irish-born James Hoban for the kind of mansion the gentry were building near Dublin at the time. The new house wasn't finished soon enough for Washington to live in; his successor John Adams only had four months of his term left when he moved in. Jefferson then spent eight years here, and, though he said it was "big enough for two emperors, one Pope, and the Grand Lama," proceeded to add east and west terraces and pavilions. Later, almost every president made improvements. James Madison needed to order a complete reconstruction of the White House after the British set fire to it in the raid of 1814.

By 1948, when Mrs. Truman noticed the legs of the piano sinking into the floor and chandeliers shaking dangerously when anyone walked overhead, investigations showed that the long-suffering White House had taken all the piecemeal additions and tinkering it could stand. It had to be totally rebuilt. But the interiors, right down to the plaster, were painstakingly removed, stored, and later put back in place.

Tours, when available, enter through the **East Wing**. As you walk along the corridor lined with portraits of former first ladies, you may be able to look into the Library, the China Room, the Vermeil Room (named for its collection of gilded silver), and the elegant oval Diplomatic Reception Room with French wallpaper of 1834 printed with American scenes.

Back near the lobby, you climb the stairs to the right, just like any guest invited to a state reception, to the sparkling gold-and-white **East Room**. The first first lady to live here, Abigail Adams, who hung out the laundry in this room, would scarcely recognize it today. Largest in the White House, it's where presidential press conferences, concerts, and the weddings of presidents' daughters are held. The color scheme was chosen by Mrs. Theodore Roosevelt – her husband liked to stage boxing

White House, south lawn

matches here, and their children were allowed to rollerskate or ride their ponies inside when the weather was bad.

The **Green Room** next-door was Jefferson's dining room, where he liked to surprise his guests with new eating experiences such as ice cream, waffles, and macaroni. Since his day it has been a parlor or sitting room, and was President Kennedy's favorite. A Martin portrait shows Benjamin Franklin with a bust of his hero, Isaac Newton. John and Abigail Adams were painted by Gilbert Stuart.

The **Blue Room**, like those above and below it, is oval, making use of the curved south portico. (The president's famous Oval Office, however, is in the West Wing, and is not on view to the public.) The gilded chairs and sofa were ordered from Paris in 1817 by James Monroe. A row of presidential portraits decorates the walls. The room has mainly been used for receiving guests.

In the **Red Room**, the walls are of deep red silk. The portraits include one of John James Audubon, the naturalist and artist, here dressed in buckskin.

The **State Dining Room** seems quite austere after those rich colors, and modestly sized, but it can seat 140. The George Healy portrait of Lincoln, reckoned to be one of the best likenesses of him, was painted from photographs and memory (the artist only saw Lincoln once).

Unless invited by the president and his family, you won't see the second and third floors where the family and guest apartments are situated, including the Queen's Bedroom, where several royal visitors have slept; Winston Churchill slept here during his stay because he didn't like the Lincoln Bedroom – or Lincoln's bed.

George's salvation

The 1796 portrait of George Washington by Gilbert Stuart was saved by Dolly Madison from the fire-raising British in 1814.

On the way out, you pass through **Cross Hall**, with portraits of recent presidents. Then you exit through the marbled lobby and north portico, which is your chance at last to get a photograph of "me at the White House." (It beats the "me and cardboard cut-outs of the president and first lady" pictures that you can pose for in the street.) Walk around the outside of the fence to see the best-loved exterior view, across the south lawn, where the presidential helicopter takes off.

The Blue Room

AROUND THE WHITE HOUSE

With the massive Greek-revival bulk of the Treasury already on one side (the east), the White House collected another neighbor on the other (west) side, though it took 17 years to build (1871–1888). Ever since the Civil War, expanded government departments had been housed all over the city in crowded temporary accommodations. The plan was to cure the problem at a stroke, with the biggest office building ever built up to that time. The **Eisenhower Executive Office Building** (EEOB), has been called the "greatest monstrosity in America" (by President Truman, and he meant this as praise) and hailed as a national treasure. It was the style that so horrified many critics; they'd expected another Greek temple and instead got a hunk of French Second Empire. Long the home of the War, Navy, and State departments, the EEOB now houses some of the White House staff, the Vice-President's Office, and the National Security Council. It is off-limits to the public.

Across Pennsylvania Avenue from the EEOB, the Blair and Lee houses are for VIP guests of the president; **Blair House** was where the Trumans lived while the White House was being reconstructed. In the **Lee House**, Robert E. Lee was offered the command of the Union army at the outbreak of the Civil War. The 1859 **Renwick Gallery** has displays of the best in American craft and design and related temporary exhibitions (see page 68). The building itself is worth seeing for its lush Grand Salon and Octagon Room and their appropriate 19th-century paintings – sentimental, romantic, and mildly erotic. It was built to house the Corcoran collection, but when that grew too big it had to be moved a couple of blocks down 17th Street to a new white marble **Corcoran Gallery of Art** in 1897.

Eisenhower Executive Office Building

Lafayette Square faces the north side of the White House. Its green lawns are a traditional gathering place for demonstrators hoping to make a point with the president – or the media. Huge groups assemble for an hour or two, and eccentric individualists or the homeless sleep under tents of plastic sheet. The bronze horseman in the middle is Andrew Jackson, not Lafayette – he's in a corner.

At the northwest corner, Commodore Stephen Decatur, a naval hero of the War of 1812, had a new house built, the first on the square. In 1819, he and his wife moved in, but after little more than a year he was dead, killed in a duel with a rival officer. Designed by Benjamin Latrobe, the **Decatur House** (www.decaturhouse.org; free tours Mon 11am–2pm) was later let to foreign ambassadors and US secretaries of state. It now houses the National Center for White House history.

On the north side of the square, the 1815 **St John's Church** (Wed–Sat 9am–3pm, Tue 11am–3pm; www.stjohns-dc.org; free) is another Latrobe design; almost every president since it was built has attended once, if not regularly. It was considered the most fashionable church in the city. At one time, you actually had to pay rent for your pew. If you take a look inside, you will see the elegant white interior, the stained glass by a curator from Chartres, and the presidential Pew 54.

Washington, DC was still a village of scattered huts and muddy tracks in 1798, when George Washington persuaded his friend Colonel John Tayloe to set an example and build a town house here instead of in Philadelphia. He chose a plot on the corner of 18th Street and New York Avenue, and William Thornton, first architect of the Capitol, designed the **Octagon** (Thur–Sat 1–4pm; www.theoctagon.org; free) for him. However, someone couldn't count as there are only six sides instead of eight. President Madison moved in here after the British burned the White House (they would have burned the Octagon too only it had become the French Embassy). He signed the Treaty of Ghent that ended the War of 1812 in the elegant circular room over the entrance hall.

Back on 17th Street you'll pass more white marble, the Greek-style **American Red Cross** building, and then, at 1776 (no coincidence) D Street, the headquarters of the **Daughters of the American Revolution**. Imposing name; imposing Classical temple. The DAR, as they are usually called, are ladies descended from anyone who campaigned for American independence. They keep a museum of period rooms from different eras and states, but they're mostly known to the public for their 4,000-seat assembly hall, Washington's best for concerts until the Kennedy Center was finished.

Finally, as you reach the Mall, take a look at the 1910 OAS **Building** (the Organization of American States). Here, you will be able to see a juxtaposition of North and South American motifs – Aztec, Maya, and Inca, and reliefs of Washington, Bolívar, and San Martín.

THE MALL

This is a perfect piece of theater. Stand on the steps of the Lincoln Memorial and look along 2 miles (3km) of magnificent green, 500yds wide, to the shining white dome of the Capitol. Enough runners for a mass marathon head in all directions and at every speed. People picnic, fly kites, and throw Frisbees. Weekends see friendly soccer, rugby, and softball matches. High school marching bands assemble for parades; buses decant eager tourists. This grassy, pebble-pathed arena, the Mall, is faced by some of the world's most wonderful museums, notably many of the Smithsonian museums (see page 59) and the National Gallery of Art (see page 68).

If the Mall today is a delight, for much of the 19th century it was a mud heap, with piles of rubbish and swampy pools. The

Baltimore & Ohio Railroad built tracks across it about where the National Gallery of Art now stands. "temporary" buildings from both world wars lingered more than twenty years after the second was over. Some of the Mall had been paved over for parking lots. It was only gradually that it all began to come right.

Presidents Kennedy and Johnson battled for the beautification of the city. The debris was swept away, far more trees were planted, and major cross-streets went underground. The result

Washington Monument

is not quite Pierre Charles L'Enfant's dream come true; he had hoped for an American Champs-Elysées, lined with mansions and embassies. But the spirit is true to his vision.

The majestic white marble **Washington Monument** ❷ (www. nps.gov/wamo; free) is the focal point of the Mall and symbol of the city. It is unimaginable that anything else could stand in the place of this 555-ft (169-meter) obelisk, which perfectly embodies the nobility of George Washington himself and shines like a beacon to lead the nation. How many lost visitors, too, must have been saved by the sight of it. There's usually a line waiting to go up in the elevator. Open daily 9am–4.45pm (Labor Day–Memorial Day), until 9.45pm (Memorial day–Labor Day). Tickets are required, but are free at the nearby kiosk. Despite the small windows, the view from the top is superb.

Hanging out around the Lincoln Memorial

The Monument has recently undergone extensive renovation, and though the 897 stairs are now closed to the public, the rest of the interior is open for tours.

The monument nearly didn't turn out this way. After a competition in 1833, the winning design by Robert Mills showed a decorated obelisk rising from a circular colonnaded building, adorned with statues. It would have looked like a single candle on a birthday cake. Fortunately, tight budgets cut out the cake and left the candle. Funds were raised by public subscription, and work started on a simple obelisk in 1848. By 1854, political squabbling brought it to a stop at 160ft (49 meters) up and there it stayed for 25 years. In 1880, the Army's engineers were called in to finish the job, which they did, by 1888. You can see a slight change of color in the marble at the point where work was resumed. The first elevator, steam-driven, took 12 minutes to reach the top; the present one takes only 70 seconds.

West of the Washington Monument, walk the tree-lined path by a 2,000-ft- (609-meter-) long reflecting pool to the

Lincoln Memorial ❸ (24/7; www.nps.gov/linc; free), a Classical temple inspired by the Parthenon. Visitors here bring much in expectation and receive as much in inspiration. The 16th president, deemed savior of the Union and martyred at the very point of victory in the Civil War, is uniquely esteemed; his memorial is revered as no other. It's an extraordinary amalgam of architecture, sculpture, and literature. Congress wrangled and dithered for 50 years, but at last the site was selected ("dignified isolation from competing structures" was specified – and achieved magnificently). Swampland had to be drained and a mound created. By 1922, the memorial was finished, and the wait had been worthwhile.

In Henry Bacon's design, 36 Doric columns represent the states of the Union at the time of Lincoln's death. The 19-ft (5.8-meter) seated white marble statue of Lincoln inside took Daniel Chester French 13 years to carve. It seems to fill the chamber, but the air is one of compassion and contemplation, not power. Only the clenched left hand conveys tension. If you can, come here in the early light of the morning and again at night. The dramatic floodlighting was an afterthought; sheets of marble in the roof, oiled with paraffin to make them translucent, didn't give enough emphasis to Lincoln's face.

Not far to the northeast, in Constitution Gardens, is a much newer place of pilgrimage, the **Vietnam Veterans Memorial** ❹ (24/7; www.nps.gov/vive; free). Doubtful of it at first, Americans have now taken it to their hearts and visit it in their millions. The V-shaped wall of polished black granite, like a cut in the earth, bears the names of the more than 58,000 soldiers who died or remain missing. Beside each perfectly etched name (inscribed in order of their death or disappearance), a small cross indicates one of the missing, a diamond someone whose death was confirmed.

Never forgotten

Touching traditions have grown around the 247-ft (75-meter) WWII war memorial. Relations and loved ones leave mementoes: toys, messages, photographs, and badges, which are catalogued and kept in a museum storeroom.

A group of veterans themselves campaigned for a memorial to be built, and in 1980 Congress agreed on the site. A competition for the design brought 1,421 entries, judged anonymously. The winner, remarkably, was a 21-year-old student at Yale, Maya Ying Lin, whose parents had emigrated to the US from China. "The names would become the memorial," she said, and there is no other inscription.

The message conveyed by the monument is achingly sad, befitting such a controversial war. Disappointed, some veterans demanded a more traditional commemoration. Soon after the wall's dedication in 1982, the Memorial Fund was urged to add the figurative sculpture and flagstaff that now stand nearby. Frederick Hart's realistic group of three young fighting men was unveiled in 1984.

In front of the Lincoln Memorial, adjacent to the Reflecting Pool, is the **Korean War Veterans Memorial** (24/7; www.nps. gov/kwvm; free). Dedicated in 1995, the memorial features stainless steel sculptures of 19 life-size, heavily armed soldiers marching in the direction of an American flag. A black granite wall, inscribed with the words "Freedom Is Not Free," is etched with 2,500 images of nurses, chaplains, crew chiefs, mechanics, and other support troops who served in the conflict. It is intended to be a living memorial, honoring all those who made it home as well as the 55,000 American troops who did not.

At the eastern end of the Reflecting Pool stands the impressive **World War II Memorial** (24/7; www.nps.gov/wwii; free), dedicated in 2005 to the 16.4 million Americans who served the cause. It's more a place of reflection and rest than a traditional war memorial. A once-neglected fountain is ringed with 56 stone pillars, one for every state and territory in the Union during the war, and hand-cast gold stars on a wall flanked by waterfalls honor the 400,000 military men and women who perished.

THE CAPITOL ❺

At the east end of the Mall, the ground rises gently to a low hill – Capitol Hill. L'Enfant called it "a pedestal waiting for a monument." There, just where he intended, stands the majestic Capitol, or "Congress House," as he named it on his plan. Each of the 50 state capitals has a Capitol, too; if you confuse the two words, you'll only be doing the same as many Americans. Crowning its elevated site, Washington's Capitol is a landmark visible from most places in the city

Korean War Memorial

The original design for the Capitol was submitted by a gifted amateur, Dr. William Thornton, and in an obvious recipe for future friction, the runner-up in the competition was appointed to supervise construction. George Washington himself laid the cornerstone in 1793. Thornton's drawings showed a low flattish dome, but as the building was enlarged to keep pace with the growing nation, a taller and grander affair of wood and copper sheeting was built. National aspirations then demanded the still more impressive baroque version that you see now, inspired by St Peter's in Rome and St Paul's in London, and over 4,000 tons of cast iron – a revolutionary use of the material for the time – were hauled into place between 1851 and 1863.

Architect Thomas Walter was helped by the indefatigable Montgomery C. Meigs and his US Army engineers, who later finished off the Washington Monument and built the fine Old Pension Building. It was suggested to Lincoln during the depths of the Civil War that construction should stop and wait for peace, but he demurred: "If the people see the Capitol going on, it is a sign we intend the Union shall go on."

Placed atop the dome in 1863, the 19-ft (5.8-meter) statue of Freedom very nearly didn't make it. The American sculptor Thomas Crawford's first drawings showed the lady in the kind of cap worn by freed Roman slaves and French revolutionaries.

The Capitol building

Jefferson Davis, then in Lincoln's first cabinet, regarded this as an incitement to Southern slaves to rebel, so Crawford changed it to a crested Roman helmet. He worked in Rome, so he sent a plaster model of his creation by sea – and shortly afterwards died. The ship was caught in a storm and as it was in danger of sinking, a lot of the cargo was thrown overboard. Not Freedom. She was still there when the ship limped into harbor at Bermuda to be scrapped; she eventually reached Washington where a bronze casting was made. Bristling with lightning conductors, she's better seen from afar, up on her lofty perch, which, incidentally, moves in small circles as the heat of the sun expands the great iron dome.

The entrance to the Capitol is on the east side. The north wing houses the Senate and the south the House of Representatives. The whole ensemble looks so familiar and right that it's hard to believe that it resulted from the piecemeal expansion plans of many architects. The last, in 1960–62, substituted a new central portico and steps, the ones you climb now.

The **Capitol Visitor Center** (Mon–Sat 8.30am–4.30pm; www. visitthecapitol.gov; free) is the new main entrance to the Capitol beneath the Capitol's East Front Plaza at First and F. Capitol streets. Nearly as large as the Capitol itself, but built underground, the C.V.C. offers an orientation center, shops, a restaurant and theaters.

The Capitol (www.visitthecapitol.gov) is open for guided tours only 8.50am–3.20pm, Mon–Sat, with free passes, which are available at the "Public Walk-up" line near the Information Desk on the lower level of the Visitor Center.

You arrive first in the vast **Rotunda**, 180 ft (55 meters) from floor to ceiling and 96 ft (29 meters) across. Tours of the building lasting about 45 minutes start frequently from here, and while you're waiting, your eyes will certainly be drawn to the painting up in the dome. It's a rather weird fresco, *The Apotheosis of*

George Washington, which might well have embarrassed the subject. The artist, Italian-born Constantino Brumidi, settled in the United States and painted in the Capitol for 25 years. He finished this picture in 11 months in 1865, using the technique of applying paint to wet plaster as Michelangelo did for the Sistine Chapel in Rome – though the result is less highly regarded.

In 1877, when Brumidi was already 72, he started on the 300-ft- (91-meter-) long monochrome frieze which runs round the wall of the Rotunda about 60ft (18 meters) up. Also in fresco, though imitating sculpture, it shows scenes from American history, starting with Columbus. Only about one-third was complete when the artist had a fall while painting. He hung suspended from the scaffolding until help came, but he never fully recovered from the shock and most of the rest of the work was finished by a pupil, using his sketches. The last 30ft (9 meters) remained blank until 1953 when Allyn Cox added three more panels depicting the Civil War, the Spanish-American War, and the first flight of the Wright brothers in 1903. The best of the paintings around the walls are by John Trumbull, showing events in the Revolutionary War in which he actually served.

The middle of the Rotunda's floor is the symbolic center of the city: the street numbers and letters begin with this spot as zero. The bodies of many presidents, former presidents, and other distinguished citizens have lain in state here.

No secrets

Adams is said to have found that the unusual acoustics of Statuary Hall allowed him to eavesdrop on private conversations across the chamber. Stand on the plaque while the guide whispers, and you will find that he was right.

Next to the Rotunda on the south side, **Statuary Hall** groans under a load of bronze and marble versions of famous sons and daughters of the 50 states, sculpted by their local artists. The results are good, bad, ugly, and laughable statues; and they're all heavy. The collection now flows out along corridors and down to lower levels, as well. This semicircular chamber was home to the House of Representatives from 1807 to 1857, except while it was being repaired after the British raid of 1814. Look for the plaque in the floor which marks the spot where John Quincy Adams sat, and where he suffered the stroke from which he died.

In the north wing, the earliest part to be built, a high semi-circular hall housed the Senate. By 1810 it was split

Statuary Hall

into two levels· the richly elegant upper one, the **Old Senate Chamber**, was modeled on a Greek amphitheater; and the more intimate lower room was the **Old Supreme Court Chamber**. From the latter Samuel Morse sent the first telegraph message, "What hath God wrought," to Baltimore in 1844. In 1860, the Senate having moved to its present quarters, the court shifted upstairs, where it stayed until 1935. Both rooms have been restored to the way they looked in the 1850s. Look at the columns in the small rotunda outside. Instead of the usual acanthus, their Corinthian capitals show New World plants that were a boon to the early American economy – tobacco leaves and corncobs.

You may get a look into the **Senate and House chambers** on a guided tour, if Congress is not in session. The stylish simplicity of the chambers is impressive. The 435 members of the

Colorful blooms at the National Botanical Garden

House of Representatives don't have allocated places on the curved rows of benches. The Speaker or a deputy presides. In the smaller Senate chamber, the 100 senators have their own desks arranged in a semicircle, the newest to be elected sitting at the back. The presiding officer here is the vice-president, but he rarely stays after the opening moments (around noon) and a junior senator takes the chair. Most of the work of Congress, and the real cut and thrust of debate, goes on in committees, which meet in the morning.

Walk through the gorgeous gardens to the western steps, facing the Mall. From the top, you will be rewarded with one of the city's best views. At the base stands Washington's finest statuary group, the **Grant Memorial ❻**. This is no triumphant celebration of Civil War victory. The general almost slumps in his saddle, brooding perhaps over the huge losses and miseries that had to be endured first. The flanking groups, cavalry to the north and horse-drawn artillery to the south, convey the desperation and tragedy of battle with poignant drama and realism.

If anything, the impact is increased when small children climb up to join the bronze riders. It took the sculptor, Henry Shrady, 21 years to complete, and he died, of the strain, it's said, just before it was dedicated in 1922.

When you've finished at the **Capitol**, be sure not to miss the **Botanic Garden** (First Street and Maryland Avenue, SW; daily 10am–5pm; www.usbg.gov; free). The original intention of the national garden, which was established in 1816, was that it should be a place to collect, grow, and distribute American plants and those from other countries that might be of medicinal or economic benefit to the American people. Over the years, the garden slowly expanded until an American expedition team, returning from the South Seas in 1842, dramatically increased the plant inventory with several living species it had collected from around the world.

The burgeoning garden occupied various temporary green houses around the city and was finally moved to its present location in 1933. The conservatory and two-acre surrounding grounds now hold 26,000 plants including an impressive show of orchids, several varieties of carnivorous plants, and dozens of exotic ferns.

Across Independence Avenue, you can stroll through **Bartholdi Park**, which has a magnificent fountain centerpiece, from dawn until dusk.

SUPREME COURT

(1st and E. Capitol streets, NE) The Court is opposite the Senate, in a dazzling marble Classical temple that would have satisfied the most vainglorious of Roman emperors. Finished in 1935, after the death of its architect, Cass Gilbert, it was expected to weather to a less blinding whiteness. It hasn't yet.

The Supreme Court (www.supremecourt.gov) is a remarkable institution: it can tell the president that an act of his, or the Congress that a law it has passed, is illegal, and has the power to overrule either. It is the guardian and interpreter of the Constitution. It decides "what the law is," said John Marshall, chief justice from 1801 to 1835, whose statue dominates the ground floor hallway. The president appoints the justices and chief justice, with Senate approval. They continue until death or retirement, so the effect of an appointment may be felt long after a president has left office; there have been only about 100 justices in the history of the United States, and far fewer chief justices than presidents.

When the Court is in recess, tour guides offer an insider's look into the courtroom itself, detailing some of the more famous cases. Open 9am–4.30pm, Mon–Fri, free tours of the Court include several informative exhibits and a film shown in the theater. The windows are always curtained – light reflected in from those pristine walls would be too bright, but colored marble columns give the eyes a break. As you leave the building, look up at the pediment over the main entrance. The toga-clad figures here represent actual characters, from Chief Justice Marshall to the architect Gilbert himself.

The Supreme Court

LIBRARY OF CONGRESS ❼

(1st Street and Independence Avenue, SE) This started out

as a small reference collection for the members of Congress. After it was burned by the British in 1814, Thomas Jefferson sold his 6,487 books to the nation: he needed the money and Congress needed the library. Now with its collection approaching 200 million books, newspapers, maps, films and photographs, it's the greatest store of knowledge in the world (www loc.gov; free).

Space has always been a problem. Congress held a design competition for a new building in 1873 but then procrastinated for years. They even proposed instead to lift the dome of the Capitol, not long completed after years of effort, in order to insert a library. Finally, in 1897, the building was finished, across Capitol Plaza from the House wing. It's the last word in gorgeous Victorian opulence, and as such was vilified, until quite recently.

Before climbing the great steps, take a look at the animated **Fountain of the Court of Neptune**, with nereids and sea-creatures spurting forth jets of water. The keystones of the second-floor windows are 33 different sculpted heads of racial types from Ainu to Zulu. The foyer is jeweled with mosaics, medallions, multicolored marbles, and stained glass, the work of battalions of American artists. A gallery gives a view of the even more palatial octagonal **Reading Room**. Some of the library's greatest treasures on display in the halls include one of three existing copies of the Gutenberg Bible, the first important book to be printed from movable type, Jefferson's draft of the Declaration of Independence, and Lincoln's of the Gettysburg Address. Take a tour to see behind the scenes in the Reading Room, the **Thomas Jefferson Building**, the newer **John Adams Building** (1939, Art-Deco, to the east), and the **James Madison Memorial Building** (1980, without much character, to the south).

Behind the **Library of Congress**, the **Folger Shakespeare Library** (201 E. Capitol Street, SE; www.folger.edu; free) is a

The ornate Reading Room in the Library of Congress

monument to the single-mindedness of a millionaire collector of a uniquely American breed. Henry Clay Folger wasn't born rich, but he rose to become the head of the Standard Oil Company of New York (which survives today as ExxonMobil). As his wealth grew, he became able to indulge a love of the works of Shakespeare that began while he was a student in the 1870s and later shared with his wife Emily, a teacher of English literature. Eventually he bought 79 of the First Folios – the crown jewels to a Shakespeare collector.

Planning a home for his collection, Folger bought land behind the Library of Congress. He saw the cornerstone laid in 1930, but sadly didn't live to see the library finished. Architecturally, it's a strange hybrid, but it works beautifully: outside, a Classical shape with Art-Deco detail and sculptures of Shakespearean characters; inside, an Elizabethan **long hall** for displays of early texts, playbills, and all sorts of stage-related rarities. Don't miss the **theater**, with its high timber galleries. Plays (not all Shakespeare's) are performed regularly.

FEDERAL TRIANGLE

The Old Post Office 🚇 (1899), at the corner of 12th Street and Pennsylvania Avenue, NW, is a piece of Victorian Romanesque architecture, which doesn't fit the Classical mold of its neighbors. Its 315-ft (96-meter) clock tower is the third tallest structure in the city. The Old Post Office is a Pennsylvania Avenue National Historic Site and is due to open as a luxury hotel under the Trump empire in Fall 2016.

The original documents of the 1776 Declaration of Independence, the Constitution, and the Bill of Rights are kept in the **National Archives**, at the corner of 9th Street and Pennsylvania Avenue. As an official government repository, the Archives also has in its collection everything related to the Kennedy assassination, Richard Nixon's infamous tapes and more. However, not everything is available for view. Nevertheless, research facilities in Maryland, where the census records are stored, are a genealogist's dream and is meant for visitors to enjoy. There's also a theater with a regular schedule of pertinent documentaries.

AROUND THE MALL

OLD DOWNTOWN

In the 25 years or so following WWII there was a flight to the suburbs in most big US cities, which meant cities declined and business and shopping districts were neglected. In Washington, the area affected was between the White House and Union Station, an area enclosed by Pennsylvania, New York, Massachusetts, and Louisiana Avenues, although it is now on the upswing.

Claim to fame

The roof terrace of the W Washington DC Hotel has featured in several movies, including *The Godfather part II* and *No Way Out*.

The glamorous Willard Hotel

Start where Pennsylvania Avenue resumes its progress towards the Capitol after the Treasury. The **Willard Hotel**, at 14th Street and Pennsylvania Avenue, NW, once the city's most famous, had fallen on evil days by 1968. Its selling point, "Only a stone's throw from the White House," became an unfortunate phrase in view of the riots that year, and it was boarded up. Now it's back, millions of dollars later, sumptuously restored to turn-of-the-century opulence. Look at the lobby and walk through "Peacock Alley," where all of fashionable society once paraded and where the term "Washington lobbyist" originated. During the 19th century, this is where office seekers and others pressing their own special interests would gather with lawmakers and other government officials to schmooze.

The rooftop bar of nearby **W Washington DC Hotel** gives you the best view in the area, especially on a summer evening where over dessert and coffee you can watch the sun go down and the monuments light up.

Across Pennsylvania Avenue, **Pershing Park** beckons visitors with shade, rest, and ducks splashing in a pool that converts to a skating rink in winter. The National World War I Memorial is planned to be constructed in the park by November 2018 for the centennial of the end of World War I. In the middle of the avenue, **Freedom Plaza** is paved with an enormous rendition of L'Enfant's street plan picked out in marble and granite.

Ford's Theatre ❾ (511 10th Street, NW, between E and F streets), the scene of Abraham Lincoln's assassination on the night of 14 April, 1865, was closed immediately afterwards and became government offices. Now a National Monument, it was meticulously restored from drawings, photographs, and other records to look exactly as it did on that fateful evening. Since 1968 it has again been operating as a theater.

Some of the furniture in the theater box in which Lincoln was shot is original, and in the basement there is a **Museum of Lincoln's Life** – and death (www.fords.org; schedules vary so check online). Chillingly, you can see the coat, shoes, and gloves he was wearing that night, and Booth's single-shot Derringer pistol.

Lincoln was carried across the street to number 516, the **Petersen House**. Though the White House was scarcely more than half a mile away, the journey over rough and unpaved roads couldn't be risked. Dr. Charles Augustus Leale, who had been in the audience, probed the headwound and knew there was no hope. The president died at 7.22 the next morning. Of the furniture in the house now, only a blood-stained pillow is original.

LINCOLN'S DEMISE

Five days after Lee's surrender at Appomattox sealed the Union victory in the Civil War, President and Mrs. Lincoln and their guests were relaxing in the flag-bedecked box to the right of the stage, watching a comedy, *Our American Cousin*, when the embittered Confederate sympathizer and well-known actor John Wilkes Booth burst in and shot Lincoln. Booth jumped approximately 14 ft (4 meters) to the stage, and though he broke a leg in the process, he somehow got away. Twelve days later he was himself shot, when troops caught up with him.

If the **Federal Bureau of Investigation** (FBI) had existed at the time, its agents would doubtless have been in pursuit of Booth. Pass by their headquarters (the entire block between 9th and 10th streets, E Street and Pennsylvania Avenue, NW), which is no longer open for tours. Always a hotbed of espionage, it's no surprise that Washington has a museum dedicated exclusively to spying. To get the full undercover experience, visitors to the **International Spy Museum** (800 F Street, NW; daily 10am–6pm; www.spymuseum.org) are put under surveillance as soon as they walk through the door and are asked to assume a "cover" identity for the duration of their stay. The dominant focus is the Cold War, with exhibits on the Rosenbergs and Gary Powers, the famous U-2 spy plane pilot shot down over Soviet air space. Aldrich Ames and latest turn-coat Robert Hanssen are also represented here, along with plenty of samples of spy gadgetry. There's even a replica of James Bond's Aston Martin here, complete with tire-shred-ding device. The museum occupies a high-tech looking group of buildings near the MCI Center and features two restaurants.

At 901 G Street, the **Martin Luther King Memorial Library** (daily; www.dclibrary.org/mlk; free) is the only building in Washington from the drawing board of German-born architect Mies van der Rohe, influential in the Bauhaus movement and one of the greats of modern architecture in post-World War II America.

To help breathe life into the downtown area, the **Washington Convention Center** at Mt. Vernon Place has under its glass roof 2.3 million sq ft (210,000 sq meters) of exhibition space to attract conventioneers and other visitors. Hotels, trendy new restaurants, shops, and a branch of New York's famous Macy's department store, have transformed these once dreary downtown blocks into a favorite destination, especially at night. Washington's professional basketball and hockey teams play at the nearby **Verizon Center** (7th and F streets; http://verizon center.monumentalnetwork.com), which also doubles as a concert venue for rock bands and big-name acts.

A colorful archway, a gift of the city of Beijing in 1986, announces DC's own little **Chinatown** (between H and I streets, NW, from 5th to 8th streets), crammed with inexpensive eateries and shops.

The **Old Pension Building** (F Street, NW, between 4th and 5th streets) was originally designed to house the administration of pensions for Civil War widows and wounded.

National Building Museum

Don't be deterred by its dull name: this great brick palace is a stunner. The architect, General Montgomery C. Meigs, was the same engineering genius who finally put the dome on the Capitol. Round the walls is a 1,200-ft- (366-meter-) long frieze of terracotta soldiers marching, riding, and rowing boats in endless procession. But it's the vast interior space that takes your breath away. Eight Corinthian columns, the largest ever erected, are each made of 70,000 bricks, plastered and painted. It was claimed that only a presidential inaugural ball or a thunderstorm could fill the void. There have been many of the first: a thunderstorm has yet to be arranged. Like many one-off buildings of real character, it's often been threatened with demolition, but now as the **National Building Museum** (Mon–Sat 10am–5pm, Sun 11am–5pm; www.nbm.org) it seems to be safe.

UNION STATION ⑩

(Capitol Hill) While plenty of their staff scurry to the Metro here, not too many members of the Congress these days stroll the half-mile of tree-lined avenue, northeast from the Capitol, to take the train, either the Metro or Amtrak. A pity, because Washington's station is not only a celebration of the railway era, it has been brought back from the dead.

Finished in 1908, its granite entrance recalls Rome's Arch of Constantine. Wise words from the classics are inscribed on its upper panels. At the front, Columbus stands looking ahead in the prow of his ship, The soaring parabolic interior was inspired by the Baths of Diocletian – and outdid them.

By the late 1960s, air travel had all but crippled the old railroad companies like the C & O, Richmond, Fredericksburg, and Potomac. Union Station was a leaky mess and the streets nearby were unsafe. As part of an effort to clean up and repopulate the east end, a major restoration of the station was undertaken in the early 1980s. Even if you're not taking a train, don't miss the station, its shops, and the basement Food Mall (www.unionstationdc.com).

SOUTH OF THE MALL

With the swamps drained and the waters tamed, a half-mile-wide pool, the **Tidal Basin**, was left between the Potomac and the middle of the Mall. You can rent a pedal-powered plastic boat by the hour, which is long enough to see the sights around the banks and probably more than enough for your leg muscles. This would be the ideal way to arrive at the **Jefferson Memorial** (24/7; www.nps.gov/thje; free), whose Classical portico actually faces the Tidal Basin.

This pristine white tribute to the third president has stood at the tip of East Potomac Park, practically an island, since 1943. Its design (by John Russell Pope, the architect of the National

Gallery of Art) echoes Jefferson's own Monticello (see page 86) and the University of Virginia. The site completes a cross, with the Capitol, the White House, and the Lincoln Memorial at the other points. However, architects damned the concept as pompous and cold, dull and imitative, whereas Jefferson was lively, original, and hated excessive ceremony. Time hasn't so much mellowed the building as it has people's reactions to it.

Inside the rotunda, a giant bronze of Jefferson stands 19 ft (5.8 meters) tall on a 6-ft (1.8-meter) pedestal, but a truer memorial may be found in his words. Some of them are cut into four panels on the walls, including phrases from the Declaration of Independence: "We hold these truths to be self-evident, that all men are created equal...".

Close by is the 7.5-acre (3-hectare) **Franklin Delano Roosevelt Memorial** (24/7; www.nps.gov/fdrm; free) which is fully wheelchair accessible. Pink granite walls mark off four

The Jefferson Memorial from across the Tidal Basin

outdoor "rooms," one for each of his terms in office (1933–1945); the monument is designed so you walk through the rooms in chronological order. Large fountains and waterfalls gurgle, and scattered bronze casts depict Franklin, his wife Eleanor, and Depression-era workers standing in a bread line. Famous quotations ("There is nothing to fear but fear itself") are etched into the walls. A bronze sculpture of Roosevelt in his wheelchair sits at the entrance to the memorial.

NORTH OF THE WHITE HOUSE

The **Washington Post** (www.washingtonpost.com) conducts free tours of its building at 1150 15th Street, NW, at L Street, every Monday (appointments only). Children must be over 11 years old. You'll see the vast open newsroom with hundreds of journalists typing frenetically or talking on the phone. All the new technology is on show, along with a display of the way it was in the days of molten lead and noisy linotype machines. Telephone (202) 334-7969 four weeks in advance to reserve a place.

The **National Geographic Society**'s handsome headquarters (17th and M streets, NW; www.nationalgeographic.com) houses exhibitions as colorful and professional as its world-reputed magazine. There may be startling laser shows, videos, or a

THE COLOR OF MONEY

To learn how to make money, drop in at the **Bureau of Engraving and Printing** (14th and C streets, SW; www.moneyfactory.gov). "The buck starts here," proclaim signs on the machines that produce millions of dollars a day in assorted greenbacks, mostly the $1 Washington portrait to replace tired old ones. Security, you'll hardly be amazed to find, is tight, but visitors can walk along glassed-in galleries, looking down on all the operations from blank paper to guillotined stacks worth millions.

mini-planetarium. **Explorers Hall** presents records and discoveries from around the world on earth and in space, with stunning photographs and models.

18th St near Dupont Circle

Massachusetts Avenue, NW has been called "Embassy Row" ever since foreign diplomats began to take over some of the stately mansions of the rich. Spare a glance for number 1775, the prestigious **Brookings Institution**, concerned with the theory rather than practice of government, a sanctuary where former or future high-level government advisors can do high-level research. The group of streets around nearby **Dupont Circle** is the closest thing Washington has to Greenwich Village in New York; bookshops, bike shops, and delicatessens alternate with exclusive clubs. A popular neighborhood for shopping, it's also the focus of the city's gay nightlife.

The **Phillips Collection** (1600 21st Street, NW; www.phillips collection.org), one of the world's greatest personal art galleries (see page 73), is just off the avenue. Opposite, the **Anderson House** (2118 Massachusetts Avenue, NW) is the palatial home of the Society of the Cincinnati (descendants of Continental officers of the Revolutionary War). The house's interior is overwhelmingly opulent, and is open to the public (Tue–Sat 10am–4pm, Sun noon–4pm; www.societyofthecincinnati.org; free).

At 23rd and P streets near the Dumbarton Bridge over Rock Creek to Georgetown, see the dark, moody **statue** of the Ukrainian poet-hero Shevchenko. For more magnificent sculpture, walk to the next bridge, at Q Street, which has four bronze buffaloes. At **Sheridan Circle** the Civil War general on horseback

Grand Dunbarton House

seems to be waving on the traffic with his hat. Farther up Massachusetts Avenue, at number 2551, the **Islamic Center** and mosque impart a flavor of the Middle East.

Even farther up Massachusetts Avenue, the **British Embassy** is by Sir Edwin Landseer Lutyens.

GEORGETOWN ⑪

A little tobacco port stood on the Potomac for over 40 years before the new capital was built next door with the clear intention of eventually gobbling it up. Georgetown, in the District of Columbia from the start, is now governed as part of the big city, but there's no way in which its identity has been submerged. Or, rather, identities in the plural, for Georgetown is quiet, tree-lined streets of little brick or weatherboard houses; gracious mansions in huge gardens; and packed cafés and noisy discos spilling crowds into the streets in the small hours. Sadly, many quaint, small stores have been driven out by the chains, and on evenings and weekends, it's maddeningly crowded with pedestrian and street traffic.

Wisconsin Avenue and M Street are the noisy, commercial face of Georgetown, lined with shops and restaurants that may only survive for a matter of months before giving way to the next contender. For contrast, walk in the more tranquil streets east and west of Wisconsin Avenue, where you will often feel as if you're in 18th-century England. Actually, the only pre-Revolutionary house, it is thought, is the solid **Old Stone House** (daily 11am–6pm; www.nps.gov/olst; free) back on M Street.

Everything from a goldsmith's to a used car lot in its time, it has been restored to the way it might have looked in the 1790s, complete with guides in costume.

Two of the larger houses on the northern fringe of Georgetown are open to visitors. **Dumbarton House** (2715 Q Street; Tue–Sun 11am–3pm; www.dumbartonhouse.org; free), built about 1800, didn't always stand on the present spot; in 1915 it was moved here on rollers, pulled by a horse from its original site 50 ft (16 meters) down the hill. Now it holds a fine collection of 18th- and 19th-century furniture and memorabilia of the Washington family.

Don't confuse it with **Dumbarton Oaks** (1703 32nd Street, NW; www.doaks.org; museum free, gardens charge). The 1944 conferences that led to the birth of the United Nations took place here. Music-lovers may recall the concerto Stravinsky named after it to mark the 30th wedding anniversary of the owners, Mr and Mrs Robert Woods Bliss. Their tastes extended

THE C & O

Since rocks and rapids made the Potomac impassable above Georgetown, the obvious thing (before railways) was to cut a canal inland. The rather grandly named **Chesapeake & Ohio Canal** (the "C & O") was started in 1828, but construction stopped in 1850 and it never reached the Ohio River. Abandoned in 1923, it was finally restored by 1961 as one of the finest recreational areas that Washington possesses. Its towpath is perfect for cycling or walking, and you'll see everything from canoes to mule-drawn tour barges on the water. Go as far as you have time for – the whole 184-mile (296-km) length is a national park. Hour-long rides on a restored canal barge, narrated by a costumed guide, which departs from 1057 Thomas Jefferson Street, April through October (tel: 202-653-5190) are also available.

from Byzantine and pre-Columbian art to landscape gardening, and Dumbarton Oaks still houses their collections and libraries (though they were bequeathed to Harvard University). Eight circular glass pavilions by architect Philip Johnson contain Mexican and Central- and South-American gold and other precious objects. It would be hard to imagine a more perfect setting. The formal gardens are 10 acres (4 hectares) of paradise, terraced above Rock Creek, dotted with pools, a theater, arbors, and statues. The garden gate is at 31st and R streets. Pick up the map of the gardens, or you'll get lost.

FURTHER NORTHWEST

Like a great slash in the earth, the valley cut by Rock Creek splits Washington into the "northwest" and "The Rest," no matter what street numbers say to the contrary. The tumbling stream can turn into a torrent after rain, and it's vigorous

The National Cathedral

enough to have run several watermills in the old days. **Rock Creek Park** (www.nps.gov/rocr) goes all the way from Maryland to the Potomac, more than 10 miles (16km) by road or track. In places a mile or more across, it narrows to a gorge where bridges cross over to Georgetown. Some of the facilities include separate trails for hikers, bikers, and horseback riders; vestiges of Civil War defenses; picnic areas; an open-air theater; tennis courts; and a public golf course. You can see wheat or oats being ground, and buy a bag of flour at **Peirce Mill** (Beach Drive near Tilden Street; www.nps.gov/pimi), restored after years of standing derelict. The Art Barn next door is a cheerful picture gallery and workshop.

One of the oldest national parks in the world (it celebrated its 125th anniversary in 2015), Rock Creek Park controls 1,800 acres (729 hectares) of green. Most of it is woodland, but the fields are cared for by the "Meadows" program, which has greatly influenced the increase in the diversity of species, whether plants, insects, or birds.

The **Zoo**, as everyone calls the Smithsonian's National Zoological Park (3001 Connecticut Avenue, NW; daily 6am–8pm; www.nationalzoo.si.edu; free), is cleverly laid out along the slopes down to Rock Creek. The animals have their privacy among the trees, and plenty of shade and water: the river, hillsides, and woods make it almost jungle-like in places. The zoo got its start with animals that were presented to the Smithsonian, which then obtained this site in the leafy suburbs in 1889. Early in the fields of preservation of endangered species and of animal health, this zoo has always been keen to educate visitors and on weekends, study programs for children are "hands-on" – up to a point. In the heat of summer, it's best to go early in the morning (around 8am) to see animals out-of-doors.

Cathedrals are intended to be seen. With high-rises banned, except for the Capitol and Washington Monument, the

Washington National Cathedral (Wisconsin and Massachusetts Avenues, NW; multiple tours available; www.cathedral.org; Sun free) stands out more than most, on its 400-ft (122-meter) ridge. It has taken most of the 20th century to build. Perhaps the surprise is not so much the Gothic style, but the authenticity. This is no copy or pastiche: it's one of the biggest cathedrals on earth, but more than that, the same craftsmanship has been devoted to it as to its 14th-century forebears. Notice the stone-carving, the gargoyles, and the flying buttresses (the best view is from the seventh floor in the west end towers). The stained-glass windows are too brilliantly clear to rival Chartres, but here on the south side you'll find one commemorating the 1969 Apollo XI mission to the moon.

Hillwood (4155 Linnean Avenue, NW; Tue–Sun 10am–5pm; $18 for adults, $15 for seniors, and $10 for students; www.hillwoodmuseum.org) is the hidden treasure of the northwest. Advance reservations are not necessary, but they are advised in May when the forests of azaleas, the gardens' foundation, are in bloom (tel: 202-686-5807). The house has the finest collection of Russian decorative arts in the west. Watch for the masterworks made by the jewelers of the Fabergé workshops, including the famed eggs made for the Imperial family.

Hillwood's grounds contain three smaller museums. A Russian-style wooden **dacha** contains a much smaller Russian collection. A modern log cabin holds Mrs Post's high quality American Indian artifacts, and another museum annex houses C. W. Post's mainly Victorian furniture and memorabilia. There's a nice café here with sit-down service, handy since the neighborhood is residential and there are not much else nearby.

MUSEUMS

Washington D.C.'s museum count reaches a dozen on the Mall alone, if you number the components of the Smithsonian separately – as you should – and take the National Gallery of Art's West and East buildings as distinct courses. Don't try to bite off too much in one day, and remember that there are more collections away from the Mall, such as the American Art Museum and National Portrait Gallery (two museums in one building), National Postal Museum, and Renwick Gallery.

SMITHSONIAN MUSEUMS

James Smithson, a British scientist, admired the United States from afar, and, on his death in 1829, he left over

Aerial view down the Mall

half a million dollars – an incredible sum at the time – "to found at Washington, under the name of the **Smithsonian Institution**, an establishment for the increase and diffusion of knowledge among men." Congress debated until 1846 before honoring his wishes.

Today, the majority of the museums lining the Mall come under the Smithsonian banner, the main exception being the National Gallery of Art. All are open every day but 25 December, from 10am to 5.30pm, except for the American Art Museum and Portrait Gallery which are open from 11.30am to 7pm. Amazingly, all of the Smithsonian museums are still free of charge.

The first Smithsonian Institution Building, known as "**The Castle**," is the red sandstone off-balance oddity that sticks out into the Mall looking like a Romanesque church. Finished in 1857, it once contained everything and everyone to do with the institution: now it houses offices, Smithson's tomb, the **Smithsonian Information Center** (open daily from 8.30am to 5.30pm), and a little cafe. Call their main number (202) 633-1000 with any questions and for a schedule of changing exhibits, or visit www.si.edu.

ARTS AND INDUSTRIES BUILDING

The building houses exhibits from the 1876 Centennial Exposition held in Philadelphia which US and foreign participants gave to the nation – mainly to avoid the expense of shipping them home. Located on the Mall between Independence Avenue and Jefferson Drive, SW, at 9th Street, the building will reopen after major renovations in early 2016 as an exclusive special events venue; www.si.edu/Museums/arts-and-industries-building.

FREER/SACKLER GALLERY OF ART

The Freer Gallery is the home of a magnificent array of Oriental art, stamped forever with the fastidious personality of Charles Lang Freer, Detroit railroad tycoon and philanthropist. He laid down the conditions that there could be no loans either from or to "his" museum, nothing could be sold, and very little bought. Although the gallery boasts some of the finest known **Chinese porcelain** and **Islamic painting**, many people go to the Freer primarily to see the famed **Peacock Room**, painted by the American artist James McNeill Whistler, who was a great friend of Freer. Whistler created the Peacock Room for an earlier patron in London to house his ravishing picture *The Princess from the Land of Porcelain*. When Freer bought the room, he had it transported to Washington lock, stock, and barrel. Continue through the underground passage

The Peacock Room in the Freer Gallery of Art

that connects the Freer to the Arthur M. Sackler Gallery (see page 60), which is full of Oriental treasures. Together, the collections in these two museums form the Smithsonian's Museum of Asian Art. On the Mall at Jefferson Drive, SW, at 12th Street; The Freer Gallery is closed for renovation until summer 2017; www.asia.si.edu.

HIRSHHORN MUSEUM AND SCULPTURE GARDEN ⑫

This museum houses the collection formed by Joseph H. Hirshhorn, a man with a mania for art. If he liked it, he bought it and he formed a large – 4,000 paintings, 2,000 pieces of sculpture – of anyone before or since. Then he gave it to his adopted country (Hirshhorn was Latvian), on condition that a museum bearing his name be built. That was in 1966, but he kept on collecting, and when he died in 1981, he left the museum another 6,000 works of art.

Paintings, only a small fraction of the collection at any one time, hang in the windowless (but for one long slit) outer rings of galleries. The bias is towards the modern, adventurous, and American: Avery, Noland, Stella. Nobody likes them all, though most experts agree that Hirshhorn's eye for good sculpture was almost infallible. The pieces are arrayed in the inner rings, bathed in the natural light from the circular courtyard (the hole in the "doughnut"). Look for the little bronzes by artists better known for their painting: Degas, Gauguin, and Matisse, and a witty Picasso, *Woman with Baby Carriage.*

More monumental works are on the plaza outside, and down in the **Sculpture Garden** across Jefferson Drive. It's a perfect setting, with flowering shrubs, fountains, and lawns, for Rodin's colossal *Balzac* and *The Burghers of Calais,* Henry Moore's strange seated figures, and a luscious nude by Maillol. The Hirshhorn is on the Mall and can be entered at Independence Avenue or Jefferson Drive, SW, at 7th Street; www.hirshhorn.si.edu/collection/visit.

NATIONAL AIR AND SPACE MUSEUM 🅭

Heaven has been captured on earth here for anyone who's fascinated by the history of aviation; if you're not that interested, this amazing collection may convert you. The vast foyer on the Mall side is only a foretaste, but none other than the wood and fabric **Wright Flyer** of 1903, which made the first ever powered, manned, controlled flight, hangs in the center. It's the original, like all the exhibits, except for some spacecraft that could not be returned to Earth intact, where the back-up vehicle is displayed. The unbelievably small **Apollo 11 Command Module,** which brought back the first men to land on the moon, can also be seen.

Don't miss Lilienthal's 1894 hang-glider, 70 years before its time (in Gallery 107), World War I (209), World War 11 (205), and the Golden Age of Flight between the wars (105). On the Mall with entrances at Independence Avenue or Jefferson Drive, SW, at 6th Street; www.airand-space.si.edu/visit.

If you wish to see more, you can visit the **Steven F. Udvar-Hazy Center** in Chantilly, near Dulles Airport in Virginia. This annex to the main museum features exhibits ranging from death-defying one-seater planes to the enormous space shuttle that occupies a room of its own.

SMITHSONIAN AMERICAN ART MUSEUM AND PORTRAIT GALLERY ⑭

The Smithsonian American Art Museum and the Natio-nal Portrait Gallery, each

National Air and Space Museum

occupying half of the Old Patent Office building on 8th Street, NW, are two of the best off-the-Mall Smithsonian museums. Smaller scaled and thus doable in an afternoon, the **American Art** side features ornamental furniture, folk-art paintings and sculpture, photos and drawings. There's a huge outline of the US in neon tubing and filled with television screens, all carrying moving and unsynchronized images relating to each of the states.

See the famous Gilbert Stuart portrait of Washington in the **Portrait Gallery** side, part of the presidential portraits collection. Sports figures, writers, photographers, business leaders – anyone who's made a mark on American life has a portrait here. Best of all is the top-floor Lunder Conservation Center (off the Mall on 8th Street between F and G streets, NW; www.

americanart.si.edu and www.npg.si.edu), a glassed-in lab where you can watch the conservators at work at five different studios, restoring the collections' treasures. There is a nice café in the building's courtyard.

NATIONAL MUSEUM OF AMERICAN HISTORY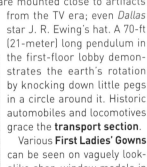

This institution has become so lively that some serious minds are a little bit shocked. If it is really "the nation's attic" of the cliché, then the dust has most definitely been swept away; there's some sharp social comment in the exhibitions. Household objects everyone remembers are mounted close to artifacts from the TV era; even *Dallas* star J. R. Ewing's hat. A 70-ft (21-meter) long pendulum in the first-floor lobby demonstrates the earth's rotation by knocking down little pegs in a circle around it. Historic automobiles and locomotives grace the **transport section**.

George Washington at the Museum of American History

Various **First Ladies' Gowns** can be seen on vaguely look-alike shop-window models in a copy of the White House's Red Room. The odd, some say absurd, Horatio Greenough **statue of George Washington** half naked in a toga has been an embarrassment ever since it arrived from Italy in 1841. On the third floor, the real Washington's campaign tent is astonishingly preserved in the **military history** section, as well as the complete gunboat *Philadelphia*, sunk in 1776, raised in 1935. On the Mall with entrances on Constitution Avenue and Madison Drive, NW, 12th and 14th streets. Part of the west wing is closed for renovation until 2018; www.americanhistory. si.edu.

> ### Star-Spangled Banner
>
> Check out the glassed-in exhibition of the faded, tattered and battle worn banner that flew over Fort McHenry in Baltimore in 1814 during the British invasion, inspiring Francis Scott Key to write the words to what would eventually become the nation's anthem.

NATIONAL MUSEUM OF NATURAL HISTORY

This giant magnet for children starts outside with a full-scale fiberglass *Triceratops* marking the Mall entrance. Go in that way and you'll encounter a huge stuffed African elephant in the rotunda. Turn right for the **fossil halls** with dinosaur – large and small – skeletons, and life-like models (the National Fossil Hall is closed for renovation until 2019). Dioramas give an idea of everyday life and ceremony in cultures as far flung as Easter Island and Cambodia, and, nearer to home, the American Indians.

Up on the second floor, the **Mineral World** has an encyclopedia of specimens extending to pieces of rock chipped off the moon by astronauts. Don't miss the coldly brilliant jewels in the **Hall of Gems**, with the Hope Diamond, the biggest blue diamond known to man and supposed bad luck charm for its owners. Tucked away in a corner on this floor, the **Insect Zoo** is another children's favorite. Here the specimens are alive, in cutaway transparent-sided cases: you can watch bees fly in with their loads of pollen and see them crawl right into the hive. On the Mall with entrances on Constitution Avenue, at 10th Street, and Madison Drive, 9th to 12th streets; www.mnh.si.edu.

NATIONAL MUSEUM OF THE AMERICAN INDIAN

This newest addition to the Mall is among the most popular. Three permanent exhibit spaces – Our Universe, Our Peoples and Our Lives – showcase more than 800,000 items, including archeological artifacts, art works, cultural and ceremonial objects, pottery, textiles, metalwork and more, all of it to honor the Native American peoples. A tour guide can help you better appreciate the enormous collection. Join a group in the Potomac amphitheatre, where you can often catch a live performance or demonstration of native craft. On the Mall at 4th Street and Independence Avenue; www.nmai.si.edu.

NATIONAL POSTAL MUSEUM

Once the city's post office headquarters on Capitol Hill, this grand old Beaux-Arts building was brought back from near ruin and now is the repository for all things postal. See the extensive stamp collections, plus examples of some of the early mail delivery vehicles, including three vintage mail planes hanging from the glass atrium ceiling, a walk-through railroad car and remnants from the Pony Express days. Children will enjoy the hands-on letter-writing and stationery demonstrations. 2 Massachusetts Avenue at 1st Street, NE, near Union Station; www.postalmuseum.si.edu.

MUSEUMS OF ASIAN AND AFRICAN ART

The National Museum of African Art and the Arthur M. Sackler Gallery of Asian and Near Eastern Art are joined by a dramatic subterranean concourse called the **International Gallery** which is used for temporary exhibits. The galleries are all below ground.

The **National Museum of African Art** (on the Mall at 950 Independence Avenue, SW; www.africa.si.edu) is the building with six copper domes over its entrance. The stars of this collection are the bronze and brass **castings** from Benin, made with great delicacy by the ancient lost wax method. Some are thought to be as much as 600 years old. See, too, the vivid **beadwork** from Cameroon and superb **woodcarvings** and powerful **masks** from Zaire.

You can enter the **Arthur M. Sackler Gallery of Asian and Near Eastern Art** (on the Mall at 1050 Independence Avenue, SW) through the pavilion with half-a-dozen little pyramids on top. The collection started with yet another of those magnificent donations by an enthusiast with money and vision that have so enriched the Washington scene. Dr. Sackler, a New York psychiatrist, specialized in Chinese **jade** from the dawn of civilization through modern times, as well as Chinese **bronzes**, **paintings**, **lacquerware**, and Near Eastern **metalwork**. Look for the Persian miniatures, so fine they seem to have been painted with a one-hair brush. Together with the collections in the Freer

National Museum of the American Indian

Italian art in the National Gallery of Art, West Wing

Gallery (see page 60), which you can access by way of the underground passage, the museums hold the country's treasures of Asian art.

RENWICK GALLERY
Enter this palatial red-brick gem, across the street from the White House, and ascend the grand staircase to the second floor where the paintings, covering everything from portraits to landscapes, traditional to modern, are stacked to the ceiling. The Renwick is affiliated with the Smithsonian American Art Museum (see page 63) and is mostly devoted to American arts and crafts of all strains, exhibited in rotation in the five galleries on the first floor. Pennsylvania Avenue at 17th Street, NW; www.americanart.si.edu/renwick.

NON-SMITHSONIAN MUSEUMS

NATIONAL GALLERY OF ART: WEST BUILDING ⓰
Two buildings side by side, East and West, form the National Gallery of Art. The austere, Classical **West Building** (on the Mall at Constitution Avenue, NW, between 4th and 6th streets) is fortunately warmed from within by its brilliant display of wonderful pictures. The building (built in 1941) and the collection owe a lot to Andrew W. Mellon, a member of the

Pittsburgh banking family and former Treasury Secretary. He gathered the best Old Masters money could buy in the 1920s and 1930s, including some that the hard-up Soviet Union was selling from the Hermitage, and presented them to the nation as the nucleus of a national gallery. Others followed his example: the Dale, Widener, and Kress collections helped fill the new acres of wall space. It's still beautifully uncrowded and admirably lit.

Paintings and sculpture are on the main (second) floor, arranged by country and period; prints, drawings, and decorative arts are on the ground floor. Start in the **Micro Gallery** where touch-screen monitors answer your questions, guide you through the collection, and help you plan your visit.

The **Italian Art** from the 13th to 16th centuries (Galleries 1–13) begins with icon-inspired late-Byzantine work. From the Renaissance, Leonardo da Vinci's portrait of the pensive *Ginevra de' Benci* is given pride of place. The only work by Leonardo in the United States, it's an early example: he was hardly older than his young sitter. Don't miss the vivid portraits by Botticelli, including the rakish *Giuliano de Medici*.

The 16th-century **Italian, French and Spanish Art** collections (Galleries 17–28) include numerous works of Titian, Tintoretto, and Veronese. Greek-born, Italian-trained El Greco dominates one room with his brilliant colors and attenuated figures, his *Laocoön* being one of the NGA's highlights.

Italian, French and Spanish Art of the 17th to 18th centuries (Galleries 29–34, 36–37) presents views by Guardi and Canaletto, several works by de Largillierre, Murillo and a portrait by Velázquez of *Pope Innocent X*, which caused the subject to sigh *"troppo vero"* ("too true").

The 15th to 16th centuries **Netherlandish and German Paintings** (Galleries 35, 38–41) include the macabre Hieronymus Bosch *Death and the Miser*, showing as he usually did the torments of hell, and Hans Holbein the Younger's *Edward VI as a Child.*

Dutch and Flemish Art of the 17th century (Galleries 42–51) includes examples of the genius of Rembrandt, with a penetrating self-portrait from his later life. There's also a chance to see two of the rare works of the enigmatic Jan Vermeer, *Woman Holding a Balance* and *Girl with the Red Hat,* with his magical lighting and air of mystery. Rubens is here in every size and a dozen styles to demonstrate his mastery of them all. You will also see Sir Anthony van Dyck's portrait of *Queen Henrietta Maria,* she with her dwarf and monkey.

National Gallery of Art, East Wing, Calder Collection

French Art from the 18th to early-19th centuries (Galleries 53–56) features the frothy spontaneity of Jean Honoré Fragonard in *The Swing* and *Blind Man's Buff,* a happy adult game of scarcely veiled eroticism.

The **British Art** collection (Galleries 57–59, 61) includes portraits by Hogarth and Reynolds, Gainsborough's gorgeous *The Honorable Mrs. Graham,* and one of Constable's views of *Salisbury Cathedral.*

American Art (Galleries 60, 62–71) is long on important portraits of early leaders, especially by Gilbert Stuart and Charles Willson Peale, whose son Rembrandt

Peale's 1801 painting of his brother Rubens Peale cost a whopping $4 million in 1985. There's an especially American flavor to the later 19th-century work of James McNeill Whistler, even though a lot of his time was spent in Europe. Look for American scenes by George Bellows, too, such as his *New York* (1911)

Some of the gallery's benefactors specialized in **French Art of the 19th Century** (Galleries 80–93). Two of Monet's studies of *Rouen Cathedral*, half a dozen of Toulouse-Lautrec's pictures of raffish Paris life, Renoir's enchanting little *Girl with a Watering Can* – all the greats.

While concentrating on the paintings, don't forget the tapestries, prints and drawings, and furniture and sculpture (especially Daumier's caricatures, *The Deputies*) down in the ground-floor galleries. The museum shop leads to an underground concourse with a moving walkway connecting the West and East buildings where there's a sprawling café near a glassed-in waterfall.

NATIONAL GALLERY OF ART: EAST BUILDING

The **East Building** (on the mall, between Madison Drive and Pennsylvania Avenue, entrance on 4th Street) comprises two linked triangular prisms, their edges sharp as knives, and was built by I. M. Pei in 1978. Utterly original, it still complements its Classical neighbor, using the same pristine stone. Little glass pyramids, small replicas of the one Pei built at the Louvre in Paris, light the underground walkway between the West and East buildings.

The East Building is currently under renovation and expansion with a view to reopen by the fall of 2016. During the works, a selected part of the collection, including some of Picasso's Blue Period, Modigliani's vivid portraits, Jackson Pollock's drip and splash canvases, Mark Rothko's glowing bands of

The Corcoran Collection

In 2015 the National Gallery of Art acquired over 6,000 works from the Corcoran Gallery of Art when it closed. The NGA displays some of these acquisitions in its temporary exhibitions and many of the works will later be integrated into the NGA's galleries.

color, and Roy Lichtenstein's giant "comic-book" pictures are on display at the West Building, the East Building Atrium and the Sculpture Garden.

NATIONAL GALLERY OF ART: SCULPTURE GARDEN

In 1998 the gallery opened a sculpture garden across 7th Street from the West Building. At the center of the garden is a circular fountain which is transformed into an ice rink in winter (mid-Nov–mid-Mar). Installations include Claes Oldenburg's *Typewriter Eraser, Scale X*, Marc Chagall's *Orphée* and Joan Miró's *Personnage Gothique, Oiseau-Eclair*.

National Gallery of Art; tel: (202) 737-4215; www.nga.gov; Mon–Sat 10am–5pm, Sun 11am–6pm, except Christmas and New Year's Day. Free.

NATIONAL MUSEUM OF WOMEN IN THE ARTS

This museum was first in the field when it opened here in 1987 with the aim of celebrating the achievements of female artists. The building is a former male bastion itself, a one-time masonic temple worth seeing in any case for its marble, crystal chandeliers, ceremonial staircases, and exuberant plaster moldings. See the liquid depth of the subjects' eyes in the portraits Elisabeth Vigee-Lebrun painted at the French and Russian courts. Lilla Cabot Perry, a friend of Monet, helped introduce Impressionism to the United States. Her *Lady with a Bowl of Violets* has a compelling, wistful loveliness. 1250 New York Avenue, NW, at 13th and H streets; tel:

(202) 783-9000, www.nmwa.org. Mon–Sat 10am–5pm, Sun noon–5pm, except Christmas, Thanksgiving, New Year's Day. Donation adults $10, students and seniors $8.

PHILLIPS COLLECTION ⓱

In a city of so much art, this is a favorite. Duncan Phillips was a boy when his family had this brick-and-brownstone house built. Eventually, he opened it to the public as a showcase for his own wonderful collection of pictures. By 1930, he had acquired so many works of art that he and his wife had to move out. Wings were added, but the feel of a private house remains, with artists and students to talk to, if you like. Every picture is a jewel of its kind. The vibrant 1901 Picasso *Blue Room* of a girl bathing is lit like a Vermeer. Don't miss Daumier's famous *Three Lawyers* snootily disputing, or the Klee collection, so innovative, funny, and unmistakable. If there is one blazing star in this galaxy, it

Renoir's The Luncheon of the Boating Party, part of the Phillips Collection

Torpedo at the Navy Museum

must be the big, exuberant Renoir, *The Luncheon of the Boating Party*. Tear yourself away to see Van Gogh's luminous masterpiece, *The Road Menders*, and the ethereal *Charnel Coast near Dieppe* by Monet. 1600 21st Street, NW, at Q Street; tel: (202) 387-2151; www.phillipscollection.org. Tue–Sat 10am–5pm, Thur 10am–8.30pm, Sun noon–7pm. Permanent collection weekdays: donation, weekends adults $10, students and seniors $8; temporary exhibitions: adults $12, students and seniors $10.

OTHER MUSEUM HIGHLIGHTS

The **Textile Museum** is the place to see magnificent rugs and carpets and exhibitions of the world's best embroidery. 701 21st Street, NW, George Washington University; tel: (202) 994-5200; www.museum.gwu.edu. Wed–Fri 11.30am–6.30pm, Sat 10am–5pm, Sun 1–5pm. Donation adults $8.

Next door is the **Woodrow Wilson House**, home of the 28th president and his wife after he had left office. Son of a minister, Wilson's vision for world peace after World War I led to the League of Nations, the forerunner of the United Nations. 2340 S Street, NW; tel: (202) 387-4062; www.woodrowwilsonhouse.org. Tue–Sun 10am–4pm. Adults $10, seniors $8, students $5.

Those drawn to the sea will enjoy the **US Navy Memorial Museum**, which tells the story of the Navy since the War of

Independence. On summer evenings the Navy and Marines stage free concerts and displays. 7th Street and Pennsylvania Avenue, across from the Archives, tel: (202) 380-0710; www.navymemorial.org Daily 9.30am–5pm. Free.

Across the Anacostia from the Navy Yard, the **Frederick Douglass House** overlooks the river from the top of Cedar Hill. Douglass, the tireless battler for black freedom and civil rights, lived here from 1877 until his death in 1895. The area around is now faded, but the house is elegant and filled with the great campaigner's possessions and mementoes of his extraordinary life, from slave to US ambassador. *1411 W Street, SE; tel: (202) 426-5961; www.nps.gov/frdo. Daily 9am–4.30pm, until 5pm Apr–Oct, closed Christmas, Thanksgiving, New Year's Day. Free.*

The **United States Holocaust Memorial Museum** ⑱ records the persecution suffered by millions at the hands of the Nazis. After entering through the Hall of Witness, you will be issued a "passport" with the name of a real victim of the Holocaust. Artifacts (including a boxcar used to transport prisoners), photographs, films, and eyewitness testimonies make up the permanent exhibition. An account for children ages 8 and above is on the first floor.

Though people invariably find the exhibit worthwhile, it is both emotionally and physically demanding. In the busy March–August season, the Museum distributes free timed passes for visits to the permanent exhibition. They are available at the Museum on the day of your visit (and distributed on a first-come, first-served basis beginning at 10am) or online. 100 Raoul Wallenberg Place, SW; tel: (202) 488-0400; www.ushmm.org. Daily 10am–5.20pm. Free.

ARLINGTON ⑲

The busy **Arlington Memorial Bridge**, ornamented with massive gilded sculptures, crosses the Potomac into Virginia. On this side of the river you'll find the **Arlington National Cemetery** (Welcome Center daily 8am–5pm, until 7pm Apr–Sept; www.arlingtoncemetery.mil; free) best accessed via its Metro stop (see page 131).

The green slopes of Arlington are still as lovely as in the early days when Martha Washington's grandson, George Washington Parke Custis, chose the hilltop site for his mansion, **Arlington House** (built 1802–1817, when the massive Doric portico was finished). His daughter Mary married Robert E. Lee in 1831 and together they lived here for 30 years, whenever army life permitted. It was in this house that Lee made his decision to refuse the offer of command of Union forces at the outset of the Civil War. Although he supported the Union and opposed slavery, he could not bring himself to fight against his own state. He rode south to Richmond, never to return.

The estate was confiscated and the grounds began to be used for the burial of war dead; out of this grew Arlington National Cemetery. Lee's eldest son fought for the return of his property all the way to the Supreme Court, where he won the case, but now that graves covered the hillsides around the house, he accepted compensation instead of coming back here to live. Painstaking restoration and a search for original or similar pre-Civil War furniture now gives an idea of the house in the Lees' day. Also, the guides are dressed up in period costume. Look for the paintings by Custis in the hall and the morning room – he was an accomplished artist.

The vista from the portico was called "the finest in the world" by Lafayette before much of the Washington planned by his compatriot, Pierre L'Enfant, was realized. Today L'Enfant, dismissed amid acrimony at the time, has his tomb just in front of the house, with a perfect view of the city. The granite slab is engraved with his prophetic map.

Solemn rows at Arlington National Cemetery

For many years, all members of the US armed forces and their immediate families could be buried in the cemetery, but the rate at which space was being used made it necessary to restrict that right, despite the vast area.

Near the entrance stands the **Women in Military Service for America Memorial**, dedicated in 1997, which honors the more than 1.8 million women who have served in the United States Armed Forces, from the American Revolution to the present. The complex incorporates an education center, set into the hillside just behind the memorial (there's a spectacular view of the city and its monuments from up here). The center details the history of women in the military and houses a database of servicewomen. Its glass roof is etched with sayings from famous men and women who served their country.

Walk south on Roosevelt Drive from the memorial to the **Tomb of the Unknown Soldier**. Broad steps climb to a 50-ton block of white marble. A single soldier from the US Third Infantry, the oldest formation in the United States, paces to and fro with metronomic precision. Visitors gather on the hour (also half-hour in summer) to watch the guard-changing ceremony.

Walk at will under the trees, discovering famous names: Taft, Pershing, John Foster Dulles. It's cool in summer and bright with blossom in springtime. Make your way back to the slope in front of Arlington House to find the **Kennedy Graves**. An elliptical stone terrace follows the contours of the hill and its wall is incised with words from the 1961 Inaugural Address: "Let the word go forth from this time and place... that the torch has been passed to a new generation of Americans..." Steps climb to a marble terrace where President John F. Kennedy lies below plain flagstones next to his wife Jacqueline Kennedy Onassis.

Marine Corps War Memorial

Behind them, an eternal flame flickers. Nearby in the grass, a small white cross and stone mark the grave of the president's brother with the inscription: Robert Francis Kennedy 1925–1968.

The **Pentagon**, headquarters of the US Defense Department, faces the southeast side of Arlington Cemetery, but it's ringed by freeways and not available for tours.

The Marine Corps War Memorial, better known as the **Iwo Jima Statue** (6am–midnight; www.nps.gov/gwmp; free), is outside Arlington Cemetery to the north. The huge bronze ensemble shows five marines and a sailor raising the Stars and Stripes on Mount Suribachi on 23 February, 1945, during the battle for the Japanese Pacific base of Iwo Jima. It took three more weeks to capture the island and cost 6,825 American lives. Japanese losses were four times higher. The sculpture, based on a famous photograph by Joe Rosenthal, is the work of Felix W. de Weldon. It took him nine years and was the largest bronze ever cast in one piece. Despite his heroism and the wide public acclaim, one of the Marines depicted, Ira Hayes, came to a tragic end. A Gila Native American, he ended up living in a $50 hut on a reservation after the war. Ten years after the historic battle, at age 33, he was discovered in a ditch, dead of alcohol and exposure.

Every morning at 8am a Marine color guard raises the flag, and lowers it at sunset. In summer, the Marine bands give free concerts here.

Looking back over the Potomac, the imposing concrete building you see shaped like a box is the **John F. Kennedy Center for the Performing Arts** (Virginia and New Hampshire Avenues, NW; tel: (202) 467-4600; www.kennedy-center.org). As late as 1971, when this great complex opened, Washington, DC had no real concert hall or opera house. Suddenly, in one go, there were both, plus two new theaters, and much more. The exterior may be massive, but it's hardly beautiful.

The inside is a treasury of art – gifts from half the nations of the world. Italy weighed in with 3,700 tons of Carrara marble, Sweden with Orrefors glass chandeliers, France with Matisse tapestries. Sculptures include works by Epstein and Hepworth, a brilliant bust of Shostakovich by Neizvestny, and the colossal head of Kennedy by Robert Berks. Try to come to a performance; there's a spectrum of choices every day of the week (see page 99). As you'll have come to expect in Washington, there's the usual souvenir shop and guides who will take you on a good tour. The Hall of States is dramatically

Inside the Kennedy Center

draped with the flags of all 50 states, the District of Columbia, and the five US territories. The adjacent Hall of Nations is also decorated with flags, these of all the nations with which the United States has diplomatic relations. The National Symphony Orchestra, under the direction of Leonard Slatkin, one the country's top conductors, is based here. The superb view of the city from the rooftop terrace is worth a trip to the cafeteria there.

Nearest neighbor to the north is none other than the **Watergate** hotel and apartment complex, where burglars recruited by the wonderfully named CREEP (Committee to Re-Elect the President) broke into Democratic party offices in 1972. It was the attempt by President Nixon and his advisors to cover up these "dirty tricks" that eventually led to his downfall. The multi-layered decorative appearance of the Watergate building has invited the barbed comment that it is a wedding cake, and the Kennedy Center the (rather disappointing) box in which it came.

EXCURSIONS

ALEXANDRIA

Years before Washington was carved out of the Potomac's swampy shore, Alexandria, just 6 miles (10km) south of Washington in Virginia, was a prosperous port, where clipper-ships could load tobacco. Named after John Alexander, a Scot who arrived in the 17th century, it really began to grow after a town was planned and half-acre lots auctioned in 1749. Lawrence Washington bought one, and his young half-brother George actually drew one of the earliest local street maps.

Part of the area allocated for the District of Columbia, it was returned to Virginia in a Congressional deal in 1846. Today it is a city suburb and dormitory, and looks and feels unmistakably like a town, full of history in its own right. Whether you walk alone or in a group with a costumed guide, or take the "trolley" which is really a bus, pick up a map at the **Ramsay House Visitors Center** (221 King Street; tel: 703-746-3301; Sun-Wed 10am-6pm, Thur-Sat 10am-8pm; www.visitalexandriava.com).

Actually, Ramsay House is probably older than the town, having long ago been moved by barge along the Potomac from another site. The river then came almost up to this point, and lapped at the bottom of the garden of the neighboring **Carlyle House** (121 N. Fairfax Street; tel: 703-549-2997; www.nvrpa.org/park/carlyle_house_historic_park; Tue-Sat 10am-4pm, Sun noon-4pm). This was, and after restoration is again, one of the finest houses in the town. John Carlyle bought two of the best-placed sections in the 1749 sale and resolved to build in the latest Georgian style from England. The house is on display with painstakingly researched paint colors, varnishes, floor coverings, and furniture. When General Braddock arrived in 1755 to command His Majesty's forces in the French and Indian War and plan the campaign, he did so in Carlyle's house. Fatally wounded only a few weeks later, he still left a poison pill for British rule, for it was his insistence that the colonies pay for their own defense that led indirectly to the American Revolution.

Across from Ramsay House, the old **Stabler-Leadbeater Apothecary Shop** (105-107 S. Fairfax Street; tel: 703-838-3852; www.alexandriava.gov/Apothecary), which served the town until 1933, has been preserved with its original furniture. Martha Washington used to send from Mount Vernon for medicines, and Robert E. Lee was in the shop in 1859 when he got his orders to capture John Brown after the raid on Harpers Ferry.

During the social season, George and Martha Washington would often make the trip from their nearby Mt. Vernon estate to **Gadsby's Tavern** (134 North Royal Street; tel museum: 703-746-4242; www.alexandriava.gov/GadsbysTavern), the center of city life in the 18th century. The hotel portion of the building is now a museum, but the restaurant is still in operation, serving period fare by waiters dressed for the part.

Down by the river near the end of King Street, the **Torpedo Factory Art Center** (105 N. Union Street; tel: 703-838-4565; www.torpedofactory.org), after an inspired transformation, houses the galleries, boutiques, studios, and workshops of scores of artists and craftspeople. Tapestry, pottery, painting, and sculpture in every medium, screen-printing, glass engraving, and photography are displayed and in some cases are happening before one's very eyes. One large room has good displays of the archaeology of Alexandria, including bottles and medical bric-a-brac from the Apothecary Shop. If you wish to delve further into Alexandria's history, visit **The Lyceum** at 201 S. Washington (tel: 703-746-4994; www.alexandriava.gov/Lyceum); built in 1839, the building has been a library, a Civil War hospital, a home, and an office building over the years. Today it houses a museum dedicated to the area's history.

Nearby, at the corner of N. Washington and Cameron streets (tel: 703-549-1450; www.historicchristchurch.org), is **Christ Church**, which looks as it did in the late 18th century when George Washington kept a pew here. Robert E. Lee also attended services in his younger days. The boyhood home of Robert E. Lee was located a few blocks away at 607 Oronoco Street, but the Lee family memorabilia, documents, and curiosities are no longer on display here for visitors. Before his father, cavalry general and a hero of the Revolutionary War, moved to the house in 1812, it had seen many visits from George Washington whose daughter later was to marry Robert E. Lee. The house was sold (and closed to the public) at the end of the 20th century. Across the road at number 614, the **Lee-Fendall House** stayed in the family until 1903. It still houses an eclectic collection of antiques (tel: 703-548-1789; www.lee fendallhouse.org).

Shoppers on Alexandria's King Street

There are plenty of restaurants and shops to visit in Alexandria; alternatively, take a seat in the gardens by the river in Founder's Park. If one is in port, you can tour a "tall ship" moored near the Torpedo Factory.

The curious building, like a stack of diminishing Greek temples, near the King Street Metro station is

Mt. Vernon in spring

the 333-ft (101-meter) high **George Washington Masonic National Memorial** (101 Callahan Drive; tel: 703-683-2007; www.gwmemorial.org; daily 9am–5pm). Modeled on the Pharos of that other Alexandria in Egypt, the lighthouse that was one of the Seven Wonders of the ancient world, it proudly commemorates the fact that Washington was a mason, and the first master of the Alexandria Lodge number 22. Apart from relics of this connection, you can see the clock from his bedroom which the doctor stopped at the moment of his death, and the family Bible. There's a fine view from the tower, reached by curious elevators or "inclinators" that ride up at a slight angle. As befits a building for, by, and about masons, the structure embodies all sorts of architectural features and symbols. Not all of it is serious. Children will like the mechanical toy parade on the first floor.

MOUNT VERNON ⑳

There were those who wished to make the victorious George Washington king of the new nation, but he turned them down flat, and looked forward to retirement at Mount Vernon, 16 miles (26km) south of Washington. On and off, this was his home from 1743 until he died in 1799. You'll soon see why Washington loved it so, but try to arrive early (tel:

703-780-2000; www.mountvernon.org; daily Nov–Feb 9am–4pm, Mar and Sept–Oct until 5 pm, Apr–Aug 8am (5pm).

Washington called himself a "gentleman farmer," but he was an innovative and enterprising one. He was an architect, too: his enlargements at Mount Vernon make it virtually his creation, but he shied away from anything too grand. Restrained dignity and practicality are the keynotes here.

Approach the house by passing the bowling green and trees planted by Washington himself. Inside, you'll notice authentically bright paint; researchers scraped through up to 20 layers to find it. The central hall is a passage from front to back, letting air in during the summer. The key of the Bastille has hung on the wall since 1790 (except when it has been lent for French celebrations), a present from Lafayette for spreading the message of liberty from America to Europe. All the rooms have furniture, paintings, and artifacts of the period, but two of them have some of George and Martha Washington's actual possessions. Upstairs, their **bedroom** still houses the bed on which he died, of a quinsy (a virulent throat infection) after only two days' illness. It's 6ft 6ins (2 meters) long – the general was 6ft 2ins (188cm) tall. Downstairs is his **study** and refuge from all his visitors. Here stand his fine Hepplewhite secretary-desk, his swivel chair, his dressing table, and his globe.

Outside, sit in a chair on the "piazza," a back porch devised by Washington himself, as long as the house and two stories high. Enjoy the view over broad green lawns to the Potomac below, before walking through the gardens. Look into the "dependencies" – buildings for cooking, laundering, spinning, and weaving. The workers included some of the 125 slaves employed on the estate (freed, as per Washington's will, a year after his death).

Beyond the stables on the way to the Potomac landing is the **tomb** of George and Martha. Two marble sarcophagi that could hardly be more simply inscribed rest in a brick vault, with relations' and descendants' graves nearby.

Finally, to give context to all you've seen and to get a closer look at Washington's life, including his legendary false teeth, tour the **Museum and Education Center**. Using the latest scientific techniques, scholars have assembled a true-to-life likeness of the first president. There are exhibits of household silver, period dress, agricultural implements, remnants of slave life, reminders of presidential life in the early years of the republic, and several small theaters showing quality short films. Mount Vernon is a full day's visit and you can fortify yourself at its food court or restaurant.

NATIONAL ARBORETUM

The United States National Arboretum, 4 miles (6km) east of downtown Washington (3501 New York Avenue, NE; tel: 202-245-2726; www.usna.usda.gov; daily 8am–5pm; free), encompasses 444 magnificent acres (180 hectares) of rolling hills, lakes, woods, and parkland. Springtime is a succession of magnolia, cherry, dogwood, and brilliant azaleas. October brings the fiery reds and golds of autumn foliage. There's always something to admire, whatever the season, from colorful fields of wildflowers to the disciplined bonsai collection.

MONTICELLO

As a young man, Thomas Jefferson cleared a Virginia hilltop near Charlottesville, 105 miles (169km) southwest of Washington, to build his home, giving it a name that means "little mountain" in Italian. He designed practically every feature of the house himself. Author of the Declaration of Independence, he became Governor of Virginia, Minister in Paris, then the first Secretary of State in Washington's Presidency, vice-president under John Adams, and himself the third president, from 1801–1809. It was an astonishing career, and Monticello is full of its relics. More than that, the house is marked by the originality of an endlessly inquiring mind. There are countless useful ideas and gadgets.

The setting is idyllic, the "little mountain" rising out of lush landscape. It pays to make the trip early in the day. (Monticello; tel: 434-984-9800; www.monticello.org; hours vary) There's a Visitor Center on Route 20 South near I-64, a couple of miles away, but that is best visited later, if you decide you want more details of the construction of the house and of daily life in Jefferson's time. Instead of stopping, head straight for Monticello, though you can't drive right to the hilltop. Vehicles have to be parked half a mile away; visitors can ride up in a shuttle minibus or walk.

From the first, Jefferson wanted something quite different from the fashionable "Georgian." He adopted the Palladian

Thomas Jefferson's Monticello

Shoemaker in Colonial Williamsburg

style, with a dome inspired by ancient Rome and the first on an American house. Planned for comfort and elegance rather than grandeur, Monticello grew slowly, over a span of 40 years, with many changes incorporated along the way as its owner learned of new inventions – or thought them up himself. The separate south pavilion was completed first, and it was here that Jefferson lived with his wife Martha in their early years. Martha died before he went on his mission to Paris, and when he returned, he embarked on the greatest expansion of the house.

You enter through the **East Portico**, where, if you look up, you'll see an indicator that connects to the weathervane on the roof. The **Entrance Hall** was a museum even in Thomas Jefferson's day. The antlers of stuffed deer heads were used to hang Indian artifacts brought back by the pioneering Lewis and Clark expedition across the continent, which Jefferson as president had sponsored. A cluster of five rooms in the south wing made up **Jefferson's private quarters**.

A plantation house like this needed kitchens, laundry rooms, a dairy, and stables. Instead of housing them in a clutter of outbuildings, Jefferson made use of the slope to conceal them under two L-shaped **terraces**, north and south arms to the house. Walk down to this longer slope to see how the broad eaves gave shelter to the servants and slaves below – and kept them out of sight. Notice the tunnel that connects the dependencies and cellars with the house. It is now acknowledged that Jefferson had an affair with one of his slaves, Sally Hemmings over several years; in 1998 tests confirmed that Sally's descendants carry Jefferson's DNA.

Thomas Jefferson never stopped experimenting with different plants for his gardens and plantation, which he converted from tobacco to grain. Take time to walk through the grounds: their restoration was based on his meticulous records.

You can see how Jefferson wished to be remembered if you walk down to the family **graveyard** and read the words which he himself specified should be written on the obelisk.

WILLIAMSBURG

Travel back to the 18th century in Colonial Williamsburg (150 miles/240km south of Washington), capital of Virginia from 1699 to 1780. Starting in 1926, the philanthropist John D. Rockefeller, Jr. funded the restoration of all the surviving early buildings and reconstruction of the missing ones with meticulous attention to detail and authenticity. You can walk this lively town, where the only wheeled traffic is pulled by horses or oxen. The shops all sell what they might have stocked in colonial times. In workshops and yards you can see the cooper making barrels, and a wheelwright, a gunsmith, and a cobbler at work (all dressed in period costume). You can eat in the 18th century too, Chowning's and Christiana Campbell's taverns and the King's Arms date from the 1760s.

The parish church has stood since 1715, but the original 1705 **Capitol** building and the **Governor's Palace** burned down long ago and were rebuilt.

Various tickets are on sale at the Visitor Center (101 Visitor Center Drive; daily 8.45am–5pm), covering entry to lists of houses and other buildings; pick up a detailed street map here. Call (888) 965-7254 or visit www.history.org for more information.

Jamestown, 6 miles (10km) southwest of Williamsburg on the James River, was settled by pioneers from England in 1607 (13 years before the *Mayflower* reached Massachusetts). Swampy and infested with malaria-carrying mosquitoes, at least 440 out of 500 colonists died between 1609 and 1610. Even so, as Virginia became more prosperous – mainly from cultivating tobacco – Jamestown remained the seat of government for over 90 years. Of the original early buildings, only a church tower still stands.

Just outside the National Park area, in **Jamestown Festival Park**, they've recreated the old three-sided fort, a pottery, and an Indian ceremonial lodge. Offshore float full-size replicas of the three little ships, *Susan Constant, Godspeed*, and *Discovery*, that brought Captain John Smith and the first 103 settlers.

Colonial houses in Annapolis

The 23 miles (37km) of the scenic Colonial Parkway from Jamestown via Williamsburg to Yorktown span the entire 174 years of British colonial presence in Virginia. Several of the original houses still stand: visit Moore House (tel: 757-898-2410), where the surrender terms were signed.

Pick up maps at the Visitor Center at the end of Colonial Parkway, where you can view the siege lines from the roof. The battlefield is complicated; before looking around, you may like to see a 25-minute film at the Yorktown Victory Center. For information about attractions at Jamestown and Yorktown, visit www.historyisfun.org.

ANNAPOLIS

An architectural gem, this small town sits 32 miles (51km) east of Washington, at the mouth of the Severn River. In the half-mile square of the historic center you'll find charming buildings from the 18th and early 19th centuries. At either end of East Street stand the **state capitol of Maryland** and the **United States Naval Academy**. The population explodes in summer, as Washingtonians escape onto the water. The best way to see the sights is on foot. Head for State Circle first, and pick up maps and leaflets at the **Old Treasury**, built in 1735.

BALTIMORE

Maryland's biggest city, 35 miles (56km) northeast of Washington, was the site of pioneering urban renewal projects. Downtown Charles Center breathed new life into the rundown old business district with lively shops, theaters, and cafés. Likewise, the **Inner Harbor** development transformed the once seedy and semi-derelict waterfront. Don't miss the **National Aquarium** (501 Pratt Street on Pier 3; tel: 410-727-3022; www.aqua.org; daily, opening time: 9am, closing times vary), one of the world's best. Fans of steam can see old locomotives at the **Baltimore & Ohio (B&O) Railroad Museum** (901 Pratt Street at Poppleton; tel: 410-752-2490; www.borail.org). Baseball buffs can go to Babe Ruth's birthplace at **216 Emory Street** (tel: 410-727-1539; www.baberuthmuseum.org). At **Constellation Dock** (tel: 410-539-1797) you can see the restored 1797 Navy frigate *Constellation*. Take a boat to **Fort McHenry**, which inspired Francis Scott Key to write *The Star-Spangled Banner*.

WHAT TO DO

SPORTS

Do-it-yourself exercise will come first for most visitors. Walking, jogging, or running, you'll be in the company of many Washingtonians. You'll find no better arenas than the green expanses of the Mall, Potomac Park, and Arlington, with waterside paths and famous sights along the way. Try Rock Creek Park and the Chesapeake & Ohio Canal towpath, too.

You'll cover even more ground if you rent a bicycle – the ideal method of getting around. Be sure to have a strong lock for when you leave the bike, using it to tie both the frame and wheels to a lamppost or railing. Check in any case that the rental agreement covers the bicycle against damage or theft. You'll see that most riders put on protective headgear and don't care if they do look a little silly.

Few of the central hotels, more of the outer suburban ones, have swimming pools. Otherwise, you face crowds at the public pools or at least an hour's drive to a beach on the Chesapeake Bay, and much further to the ocean beaches of Virginia.

Tennis players will find many public courts. Call the D.C. Department of Parks and Recreation at (202) 673-7646 to ask about permits to use them. Some of the private clubs will allow visitors to play (see the *Yellow Pages* of the phone book). The same applies to squash and racquetball clubs. Rock Creek Park and East Potomac Park have public golf courses, and there are more out in adjacent Maryland and Virginia. Diplomats and others in the huge foreign community have introduced various exotic sports, sometimes to the stupefaction of the locals. On weekends, in West Potomac Park near the Lincoln Memorial, you might catch a cricket match, or see some rugby, polo, soccer, or softball. Anyone here for the

Cyclists in Georgetown

longer term could contact the clubs and join in.

This isn't quite the Wild West, but you can ride horses from stables in Rock Creek Park and the suburbs. If you've an urge to get on the water, you can rent a rowboat or canoe on the C & O Canal (see page 55), sail on the Potomac, go white-water rafting on its rapids, or sedately propel a pedalo on the Tidal Basin near the Jefferson Memorial. More serious sailors will go east to Annapolis to explore the historic waters of the Chesapeake Bay. The renowned Annapolis Sailing School is at 601 6th Street (Tel. 800-638-9192; www.annapolissailing.com). In a hard winter, the C & O can freeze for skating in a scene like an old Dutch painting; there is also half a dozen indoor rinks where you can rent skates.

Washington Wizards shoot to win

SPECTATOR SPORTS

For longer than anyone can remember, the national games have been baseball and American football, with basketball and ice hockey playing important supporting roles. The seasons for each used to be as fixed: football from September to New Year's Day, baseball from April to October, ice hockey from October to April, and basketball from September to May. Now they are a little blurred at both ends, with pre-season games, play-offs, and various "bowls," but essentially the pattern remains. It's infinitely worth going to a "big game," even if you have no idea of the rules. It's all superbly organized, and a great day out for the whole family.

Robert F. Kennedy ("RFK") Stadium (East Capitol and 22nd streets, SE; www.dcsec. com/Venues/RFKStadium. aspx), once home of the home team, the Redskins, now hosts Washington's Major League Soccer (MLS) franchise, DC United. It also serves as a temporary home for the city's baseball team, the Nationals, until their huge new stadium is erected in the southeast, on the banks of the Anacostia River.

> ### The Redskins
>
> Washington's own football team, the Redskins, is one of the better teams in the country. They play home games at FedEx Stadium in Landover, Maryland. Forget buying a Redskin ticket; they're sold out years in advance.

Both the ice hockey (the Washington Capitals) and basketball (the Washington Wizards) teams play at a new downtown arena, the Verizon Center (http://verizoncenter.monumental network.com). A lot of people prefer watching college games, especially basketball, to the "pro" level, and the universities in and around Washington play some of the best.

SHOPPING

Shopping hours run from about 10am–6 or 7pm Mon– Sat, with most suburban, mall, and Georgetown shops opening their doors on Sun-days as well. Most department stores are open until 8pm on Thursdays and from 12 noon–5pm on Sundays.

WHERE TO SHOP

Washington DC has no single shopping area. Instead, they are scattered over the city and the inner and outer suburbs. The old downtown area, once blighted, has now been revived, and features several shops and a department store.

Shopping malls pack the maximum variety of outlets into big, climate-controlled spaces. Downtown, The Shops at National Place (between 13th and 14th, E and F streets, NW), and Union Station combine varied shopping and eating opportunities even more than most malls. In Georgetown, Canal Square (M and 31st streets, NW) and Georgetown Park (M Street and Wisconsin Avenue, NW) are multi-level marketplaces of boutiques. The Watergate mall, Les Champs (600 New Hampshire Avenue, NW), has some of the top couturiers at top prices, though those might still be less than on their home turf. Big selections further out of the city include the two Tysons Corner malls in McLean, Virginia. For "deep discounting," try the biggest with the most, Potomac Mills Mall, sprawling like an airport just off route I-95, 30 miles (50 km) south.

While Georgetown still has its little bookshops, galleries, antiques shops, and boutiques, upscale chain stores have taken over with a vengeance, forcing out many of the more venerable establishments. In fact, the intersection of Wisconsin and M streets, the neighborhood's ground zero, becomes a veritable parking lot on weekends. Sidewalks are packed five across, making what was once a lovely window-shopping neighborhood significantly more aggravating. Best to come on a weekday morning if you'd like a leisurely browse.

WHAT TO BUY

Books. With their massive selections, the bookstores are a pleasure to browse in; some stay open late and many have internet facilities (see page 123). KramerBooks and Afterwords (1517 Connecticut Avenue, NW; www.kramers.com) has a bookstore and café combined. The national

Bargain hunters

Sunday's *Washington Post* (www.washingtonpost.com) will give you some idea of what sales are happening where.

Politics & Prose book store

chain Barnes & Noble has several outlets in the city.

Clothes. They've got the lot, somewhere: originals from the Paris salons; some of the best American design at Polo/Ralph Lauren (3222 M Street, NW); trends that caught on and stayed, like the casual and dress-wear at Banana Republic (the corner of M and Wisconsin streets or 601 13th Street) Most of the better known boutiques are in Georgetown, but cruise the Dupont Circle area and U Street for one-of-a-kind fashion. Macy's, a branch of the New York chain, is downtown at 12th and G streets, NW, and is the city's only true department store.

Crafts. Most souvenirs masquerading as craftwork are mass-produced junk imported from East Asia. For something better, try the museum shops. Look in the Georgetown galleries, too, for genuine handmade Americana. The Department of the Interior Museum (18th and E streets, NW) has a gift shop that sells American Indian craftwork - new but in traditional styles (www.indiancraftshop.com). For pieces which straddle the boundary between craft and modern art, the Torpedo Factory

Museum shopping
All the art galleries and museums have good gift shops; they're the best place to buy your souvenirs and presents.

Art Center (105 N. Union Street, Alexandria, Virginia; www.torpedofactory.org) is a multistory mall of workshops and outlets (see page 82).

Gadgets. There's always something new in the quest for labor-saving devices, especially to use in the kitchen, the yard (meaning the garden), the pool, or the car. Look in the hardware sections of department stores or in the specialty kitchen shops. (Before buying anything, overseas visitors should make sure that any electrical goods can be adapted to their home voltage and plug system.)

Records. Discounting on CDs is frenetic – just look at the "Weekend" section in the Friday newspapers for the latest sales. When you are shopping around, notice whether you are getting a digital recording.

Stationery. You'll find a delightful array of cards, notepads, and office materials in the city, and the shops are irresistible, with their rainbow-colored displays and frequent new gimmicks. Take a look in Fahrney's (1317 F Street, NW; www.fahrneyspens.com), which has been keeping Washington bureaucrats in pen and ink since 1929 and features the finest and widest collection of writing instruments that you are likely ever to see in one place.

Wines and spirits. Through some financial wizardry, good French wines can cost less here than in France, but there are no savings on fine California varietals. Discount liquor stores have specials on spirits that make some prices cheaper than the duty-free shops at the international airports.

ENTERTAINMENT

Visitors here for only a short time need to find out quickly what's going on. Check the newspapers, especially the Friday

"Weekend" section of the *Washington Post*, the free *Washington City Paper* (which appears every Thursday; www.washingtoncitypaper.com), and *Washingtonian* magazine (www.washingtonian.com). Try TicketPlace (923 F Street, NW; tel: (202) 393-2161) for advance or half-price same-day tickets for cultural and sports events. For news of concerts and lectures, mostly free, at Smithsonian venues, tel: (202) 633-1000.

When the John F. Kennedy Center's (www.kennedy-center.org) Opera House, Concert Hall, Eisenhower Theater, and half-dozen smaller locations opened, the capital's culture scene was transformed. Now, you may see a pre-New York try out or a hit play that you missed. World-class ballet companies, touring orchestras, and soloists often include Washington in their itineraries. The Washington Opera performs for a short winter season, and the National Symphony Orchestra, transformed into one of the best in the country by cellist-turned-conductor Mstislav Rostropovitch, gives frequent concerts. Tel: (202) 467-4600 or log onto www.kennedy-center.org for a full calendar of events.

Live at the Kennedy Center

Look for other concerts – most are free – at the Anderson House, Library of Congress, Phillips Collection, Corcoran Gallery, the National Cathedral, and especially the National Gallery of

Art. And you could hardly ask for more live theater. There's the Elizabethan-style Folger Theatre, the world-renowned Shakespeare Theatre, Ford's Theatre, the Woolly Mammoth, Studio Theatre, Arena Stage, the Warner, and the restored National Theater.

On weekends, satirical cabaret is added to the menu in some bars, restaurants, and clubs. Look out for the Capitol Steps, a comedy troupe made up entirely of Hill staffers whose wicked sense of humor knows no party affiliation.

The choice of movies is vast – check the newspapers. Every suburb has several cinemas but many of the "first run" houses with the latest films are on M Street or Wisconsin Avenue (both at the Georgetown end and in the upper northwest).

Dancing is offered in bars, clubs, and discos, even afloat the Potomac in a boat. Pick your music from a range of styles as well; the biggest concentration of all varieties is in Georgetown along and near M Street and Wisconsin Avenue, with other pockets on Capitol Hill, near Dupont Circle, and in Alexandria. Note that in the entire US, the minimum legal drinking age is 21. Many clubs make that their minimum entry age as well. Don't expect any real action before 9:30 or 10pm.

Big bands at the Virginia Jazz Festival

Jazz fans kept the faith alive through the lean years; now new jazz bars and clubs have joined the long-established Blues Alley (situated behind 1073 Wisconsin Avenue; www. bluesalley.com), where you can listen as you dine.

Some of the big hotel bars have regular pianists. Pubs are livelier: some are Irish, and many have live music.

CALENDAR OF EVENTS

The city's broad avenues are made for a parade and hardly a week goes by without some sort of event involving marching bands, parade floats, and all level of dignitaries. The biggest is the **Presidential Inaugural**, which occurs **every four years** and draws thousands along Pennsylvania Avenue between the Capitol and the White House. Other main events include:

February Chinese New Year, including parade and festivals in Chinatown.

12 February Lincoln's Birthday; ceremony staged at Lincoln Memorial.

22 February Washington's Birthday Parade; ceremony (nearest Mon) at the Washington Monument.

March St Patrick's Day Parade, Constitution Avenue, the Sunday after 17 March. Kite Festival, last Saturday in March, held west of the Washington Monument.

March/April Cherry Blossom Festival; Cherry Blossom Parade, Constitution Avenue, first Saturday in April. Easter Egg Roll on White House lawn, 10am–2pm Monday after Easter.

June/July Smithsonian Folklife Festival with music, dance, crafts, food, held near National Museum of American Indian, through last week of June till first week of July.

4 July Independence Day fireworks, 9:15pm near Washington Monument.

September Latino Festival for two days in mid-September on Pennsylvania Avenue. Rock Creek Park Blues Festival takes place on a weekend in late September.

Late October Marine Corps Marathon, starting from the Iwo Jima Statue and winding through Arlington and DC.

11 November Veterans' Day ceremony, 11am at the Tomb of the Unknown Soldier.

December Christmas tree lighting ceremonies (at the Capitol and Elllpse); pageants everywhere.

EATING OUT

Eating out is a way of life for many city-dwellers. Yet, not so long ago, Washington could be written off as a gastronomic disaster. Things hadn't advanced much since President Van Buren was rejected by the electorate on suspicion of dining on things foreign and fancy instead of meat, potatoes, and gravy as a good American should. No more. Waves of food fashion have arrived. Better still, waves of immigrants with their own ideas reached the shores of the Potomac and stayed. Now, you can eat a different ethnic cuisine every lunchtime and evening for a month without duplicating. All this competition keeps prices down, too.

You can eat practically around the clock: breakfast blends into lunch, and dinner can start in the afternoon with "early bird" price reductions. Sunday brunches can be gargantuan bargain feasts (sometimes with live musical accompaniment), but you may need to reserve.

The hungry visitor, short of time and funds, will bless that great innovation, the food mall. Dozens of outlets are gathered under one roof, usually with a central area of tables and chairs. Prices are surprisingly low and there's no more than a moment's wait to collect your hamburger, French fries (chips), curry with rice and chapattis, pizza (up to two inches thick), Greek salad, moussaka, hot dogs, sushi, or fried chicken. Health food and salad bars have sprouted everywhere. In some food malls, you select a plateful of salad, which is then weighed at the cash desk; you pay on a per-pound basis. Some of the best-located food malls are: The Shops at National Place (13th and 14th, E and F streets); spectacular Union Station (see page 50); and Crystal City (at the Metro station).

The Adams-Morgan district, around Columbia Road and 18th Street, NW, is an animated area of multi-ethnic restaurants. Equally, the area around Dupont Circle, at the intersection of Connecticut and Massachusetts Avenues, is a popular spot for dining and evening entertainment.

Fancier restaurants may insist on jackets and ties for men. They can usually lend you something if you arrive without, and you may be glad of it if the air-conditioning is especially fierce.

WHAT TO EAT

Washington is a treasure trove of fine restaurants to satisfy every taste and every budget. From the extravagance of Kinkead's to the modest Pasta Mia, high quality food abounds throughout the city. There's also fine

Chesapeake Bay fresh crabs

people-watching to be done in the city's eateries where the famously powerful and the powerfully famous indulge in conversation over their cuisine.

Fresh fish and shellfish of every variety play a prominent role in Washington's menus. Some come from the Chesapeake Bay, caught and delivered daily and served at the height of their freshness and flavor. Oysters, scallops, crabs, and clams are especially good and are not to be passed up.

Historic touches from the North and South have found their way onto menus in interesting and delectable ways. Chowders, gumbos, soups, and stews are thick and filling and, more often than not, owe their inspiration to regional American cookery. These crowd pleasers can turn up as hearty main courses or "dressed up" and served as fancy starters.

An eclectic selection of scrumptious dessert fare is common in many Washington restaurants. Strawberry shortcake (with baking powder biscuits), key lime pie, interesting variations of cheesecake, and luscious fruit-filled pies are some of the tempting treats featured. Save room for these worthy finales.

Perhaps it seems strange that a visit to the US capital should be one's chance to try Afghan or Ethiopian food. Italian cooking arrived long ago, but became debased into spaghetti and meatballs. Now its focus has sharpened into more authentic and regional dishes. Something similar has happened to the other old-established import, Chinese cuisine. It's still mainly centered in Chinatown (H and I streets, NW, from 5th to 8th streets), but instead of just Cantonese modified to American tastes, customers are demanding and getting genuine dishes from Szechuan, Peking, and Hunan as well.

Enthusiasm for Thai food has spread around the world; naturally Washington joined in. Restaurants have set up alongside the established French on and off K Street, NW, between 18th and 21st streets, and others are dotted all over the city. Vietnamese cuisine has also proliferated in Washington over the past few decades, a boon for DC diners. Healthy, light, and appetizing, the food comes in generous portions. If you crave still more variety, there's every kind of Latin American, Middle Eastern, Indian, and dozens of different European restaurants. Nearly always, the cooks have arrived with the cuisine.

Desert at Matchbox Pizza Bistro

PLACES TO EAT

Unless otherwise noted, restaurants below accept major credit cards (American Express, MasterCard, and Visa).

$$$$ = $20–25 (per entree)   **$$$** = $15–19
$$ = $10–14   **$** = Below $10

CAPITOL HILL AND UNION STATION

Dubliner $$ *520 N. Capitol Street, NW; tel: (202) 737-3773;* www. dublinerdc.com. Lunch, dinner daily. Smoky Irish pub and a favorite of those who live and work on Capitol Hill. Staple traditional fare includes fish and chips, shepherd's pie, and beef stew. Live music every night, and a wide range of lagers and ales. Metro: Union Station.

Hawk and Dove $$–$$$ *329 Pennsylvania Avenue, SE; tel: (202) 547-0030;* www.hawkndovedc.com. Lunch, dinner daily, breakfast on weekends. Old-line Capitol Hill hangout frequented by staffers and congressmen. Excellent burgers and a good choice of brews. Metro: Union Station.

Jimmy T's $ *501 East Capitol Street, SE; tel: (202) 546-3646.* Breakfast and lunch Tue–Sun; closed Mon. Eccentric diner with mismatched dishware, which is very popular with the locals. Enjoy waffles, omelets, fried eggs, grilled sandwiches, and milkshakes. Expect to wait in a line on weekend mornings. Cash only. Metro: Union Station.

Montmartre $$ *327 7th Street, SE; tel: (202) 544-1244;* www.mont martredc.com. Lunch Tue–Fri, dinner Tue–Sun, brunch Sat–Sun. Closed Mon. Authentic French food with an extensive wine list. French owner and staff. Busy but delicious Sunday brunches. Metro: Eastern Market.

Ted's Bulletin $$$ *505 8th Street, SE; tel: (202) 544-8337,* www. tedsbulletin.com. Breakfast, lunch, dinner daily. Large, delicious, reasonably priced servings. Home-made tarts are excellent and "adult" milkshakes –really mouthwatering. Metro: Eastern Market.

Tortilla Cafe $$ *210 7th Street, SE; tel: (202) 547-5700; www.tortilla cafe.com.* Lunch and dinner daily. Small, simply furnished restaurant serving excellent authentic Mexican and Salvadoran food. Fast and friendly service. Great value for money. Metro: Eastern Market.

We the Pizza $$ *305 Pennsylvania Avenue, SE; tel: (202) 544-4008; www.wethepizza.com.* Lunch and dinner daily. Huge selection of pizzas and cast iron pies. Service is quick and free refills of drinks are offered. Metro: Eastern Market.

DOWNTOWN

15 Ria $$$ *DoubleTree by Hilton Hotel Washington, 1515 Rhode Island Avenue, NW; tel: (202) RIA-0015; www.15ria.com.* Breakfast, lunch and dinner daily. A warmly decorated dining room serving a wide choice of American upscale comfort food with specials such as steak, suckling pig and whole 'fish of the moment.' Good selection of micgrobrews and bourbons at the bar. Metro: Dupont Circle.

Cafe Mozart $$ *1331 H Street, NW; tel: (202) 347-5732; www.cafe mozartdc.com.* Open every day. Casual, homey, and offering authentically European fare, which features *kielbasa*, *knockwurst*, warm potato soup, and an extensive beer selection. Lunch specials are a bargain. Metro: Metro Center.

Capital Grille $$$$ *601 Pennsylvania Avenue, NW; tel: (202) 737-6200; www.thecapitalgrille.com.* Lunch, dinner Mon–Fri; dinner only Sat–Sun. For serious carnivores. Steaks are huge, aged in a see-through meat locker. Customers are mainly cigar-chomping conservatives. Metro: Archives-Navy Memorial.

Capitol City Brewing Co. $$ *11th and H streets, NW; tel: (202) 628-2222. NW; tel: (202) 628-2222; www.capcitybrew.com.* Lunch and dinner daily. A brew pub that offers several homemade microbrews on tap and a traditional menu of burgers, sandwiches, salads and fries. There's another branch at Union Station. Metro: Metro Center.

DC Coast $$/$$$ *The Tower Building, 1401 K Street, NW; tel: (202) 216-5988; www.dccoast.com.* This impressive Art Deco building provides a perfect setting for some innovative West Coast and Pacific Rim cuisine. Fine wine list and draft beers from around the world. Metro: Farragut North.

Georgia Brown's $$$ *950 15th Street, NW; tel: (202) 393-4499;* www.gbrowns.com. Lunch, dinner Mon–Fri; dinner only Sat; brunch, dinner Sun. Upscale Southern dishes are served with a twist on the classics: fried chicken, biscuits (savory scones) and gravy (white sauce), and smothered pork chops. Comfortable sofa-style booths, and a live jazz trio accompanies Sunday brunch. Metro: McPherson Square.

Jaleo $$$$ *480 7th Avenue, NW; tel. (202) 628-7949;* www.jaleo.com/dc. Lunch, dinner daily. Trendy tapas place where the wait for a table usually exceeds 90 minutes. Accepts no reservations. Metro. Archives-Navy Memorial.

Luke's Lobster $$ *624 E Street, NW; tel: (202) 347-3355;* www.lukeslobster.com. Lunch and dinner daily. Maine-style menu: very tasty lobster, crab and shrimp rolls and bisque and chowder. Good soups. Metro: Gallery Place.

McCormick & Schmick's Seafood $$$ *1652 K Street, NW; tel: (202) 861-2233;* www.mccormickandschmicks.com. Lunch, dinner daily. Fish and crustaceans of every variety excellently prepared and served by a knowledgeable waitstaff. Salmon and rockfish are especially good. Metro: Farragut North. There is another branch at 9th and F streets, NW, tel: (202) 639-9330, near the Spy Museum. Metro: Gallery Place.

Occidental Grill $$$ *1475 Pennsylvania Avenue, NW; tel. (202) 783-1475;* www.occidentaldc.com. Lunch, dinner daily. Old-line clubby watering hole serving inventive sandwiches and meat-and-potatoes dishes done to perfection. Metro: Metro Center, Federal Triangle.

Old Ebbitt Grill $$–$$$ *675 15th Street, NW; tel (202) 347-4800;* www.ebbitt.com. Open daily lunch and dinner; Sunday brunch. Established 1856 and a block from the White House, this long-time favourite serves American cuisine with an emphasis on seafood and burgers. Reservations a must. Metro: Metro Center.

Rasika $$$$ *633 D Street, NW; tel: (202) 637-1222;* www.rasika restaurant.com. Lunch and dinner Mon–Sat. Chef Vikram Sunderam's modern take on Indian cuisine. Pricy but delicious Tawa, Sigri and Tandoori dishes. Temperature controlled wine cellar. Metro: Archives-Navy Memorial.

Slipstream $$ *1333 14th Street, NW; tel: (202) 450-2216;* www.slip streamdc.com. Breakfast, lunch, dinner. Excellent crafted coffee and cocktails, a lot of great breakfast and lunch options, including vegetarian ones. Metro: Farragut North.

Teasim $–$$ *400 8th Street, NW; tel: (202) 638-6010;* www.teaism. com. Breakfast, lunch, dinner daily. Japanese inspired menu features *bento* boxes and a wide selection of freshly brewed teas. Order your meal at the counter and enjoy in the minimalist dining room. Metro: Archives-Navy Memorial. Another branch at 2009 R Street NW, near Dupont Circle, tel: (202) 667-3827.

Zaytinya $$$ *701 9th Street, NW; tel: (202) 638-0800;* www.zay tinya.com. Lunch and dinner daily. Brunch Sat–Sun. Renowned chef José Andrés offers innovative mezze menu inspired by Turkish, Greek and Lebanese cuisines. Unique Mediterranean wines. Metro: Gallery Place.

FOGGY BOTTOM & GEORGETOWN

1789 $$$$ *1226 36th Street, NW; tel: (202) 965-1789;* www.1789 restaurant.com. Dinner daily. Situated in a Federal-style townhouse with a nouveau-American menu. Long-time favorite and among the city's best. Decorated at Christmas; excellent for special occasions.

Bistro Francais $–$$ *3124 M Street, NW; tel: (202) 338-3830;* www.bistrofrancaisdc.com. Lunch, dinner daily. Open till 4am. This French restaurant is an excellent place to come if you want a bite to eat after a night on the town. Try the lamb, onion soup, or omelets.

Booeymonger $ *3265 Prospect Street, NW; tel: (202) 333-4810;* www.booeymonger.com. Open daily. This is primarily a students' haunt. Good place for a big breakfast. Excellent deli sandwiches and espresso bar.

Clyde's of Georgetown $$ *3236 M Street, NW, tel. (202) 333-9180; www.clydes.com.* Lunch and dinner daily. Authentic American dining in a nice traditional saloon ambiance. Menu based mainly on local produce. Appetizing home-made desserts. Metro: Roslyn.

Founding Farmers $$$ *1924 Pennsylvania Avenue, NW; tel: (202) 822-8783; www.wearefoundingfarmers.com.* Breakfast Mon–Fri, dinner daily, brunch weekends. Restaurant specializing in high-quality healthy foods. Mainly American fare. Delicious fried green tomatoes, pot roast and mussels. Reservations recommended as it gets really busy at times. Metro: Foggy Bottom.

Marcel's by Robert Wiedmaier $$$$ *2401 Pennsylvania Avenue, NW; tel: (202) 296-1166; www.marcelsdc.com.* Dinner daily. Seasonal menu of French and Flemish cuisine from the highly-acclaimed chef and proprietor, Robert Wiedmaier. The largest selection of Belgian beer in town. Reservations highly recommended. Jacket required. Metro: Foggy Bottom.

Martin's Tavern $$ *1264 Wisconsin Avenue, NW; tel: (202) 333-7370; www.martinstavern.com.* Lunch, brunch and dinner daily. Open until late at night. Established in 1933, a real Georgetown landmark restaurant/pub still serves excellent American fare. John F. Kennedy proposed to Jacqueline here and many U.S. Presidents have come to dine here too.

Prime Rib $$$$ *2020 K Street, NW; tel: (202) 466-8811; www.theprimerib.com.* Lunch, dinner Mon–Fri, dinner only on weekends. A DC institution with tuxedoed waiters serving dependably excellent prime rib, accompanied by music from the baby grand piano. Metro: Foggy Bottom.

Sequoia $$$ *Washington Harbour, 3000 K Street, NW; tel (202) 944-4200; www.arkrestaurants.com/sequoia.* Lunch, dinner daily. This riverside restaurant serving American fare has an enormous menu and beautiful city views from the terrace. Excellent place for Sunday brunch.

ADAMS MORGAN & DUPONT CIRCLE

i Ricchi $$$–$$$$ *1220 19th Street, NW; tel: (202) 835-0459;* www.i
ricchidc.com. Lunch, dinner Mon–Sat; closed Sun. This Tuscan grill
attracts the rich and famous. Fish, steaks seasoned with rosemary,
plus lamb, beef and shrimp are standouts. Metro: Dupont Circle.

Kramerbooks and Afterwords Cafe $ *1517-21 Connecticut Avenue,
NW; tel: (202) 387-3825.* Open daily; cafe open 24 hours on week-
ends. Convivial café and bookstore, where you can enjoy a late-
night dessert and coffee. Metro: Dupont Circle.

Nora $$$$ *2132 Florida Avenue, NW; tel: (202) 462-5143;* www.noras.
com. Dinner Mon–Sat; closed Sun. Organic ingredients carefully
prepared and served in an elegant townhouse. Metro: Dupont Circle.

Pasta Mia $ *1790 Columbia Road, NW; tel (202) 328-9114.* Dinner
daily. Popular red-checked tablecloth restaurant where you can
invent your own pasta dish. Generous portions.

Tabard Inn $$–$$$ 1739 N Street, NW; tel: (202) 331-8528.
Lunch, dinner daily; Sun brunch. An eclectic menu that includes
everything from crab cakes to potato cakes. Peaceful garden and
a flea-market mix of furnishings. Metro: Dupont Circle.

ALEXANDRIA

Gadsby's Tavern $$$ *138 N Royal Street; tel: (703) 548-1288;* www.
gadsbystavernrestaurant.com. Lunch, dinner daily. Favorite spot
of George Washington's, authentically restored and serving 18th-
century recipes.

La Madeleine French Bakery and Cafe $–$$ *500 King Street;
tel: (703) 739-2854;* www.lamadeleine.com. Lunch, dinner daily.
French country cuisine served cafeteria-style and featuring roast-
ed chicken and quiches.

Mount Vernon Inn $$–$$$ *at the Mount Vernon estate; tel: (703)
780-0011;* www.mountvernon.org/inn. Lunch, dinner daily. Ele-

gantly prepared American fare includes colonial favorites such as venison, plus seafood and beef. Tour the mansion first, then dine.

BALTIMORE

Charleston Restaurant $$$$ *1000 Lancaster Street; tel: (410) 332-7373;* www.charlestonrestaurant.com. Next to Harbor East Marina. Dinner Mon–Sat. An exquisite complete dining experience in elegant formal ambiance. Creative, eclectic, menu.

Dalesio's Restaurant $$$ *829 Eastern Avenue; tel: (410) 539-1965;* www.dalesios.com. Lunch, dinner Mon–Sat, on Sun dinner only. Little Italy's restaurant offers tasty and reliable Italian fare.

CHARLOTTESVILLE

C&O Restaurant $$$ *515 E Water Street; tel: (434) 971-7044;* www.candorestaurant.com. Lunch, dinner Mon–Fri; dinner only Sat–Sun. Unpretentious but excellent French, Cajun and Thai inspired menu. The upstairs dining room is more formal.

Silver Thatch $$$ *3001 Hollymead Drive; tel: (434) 978-4686;* www.silverthatch.com. Dinner Tues–Sat; closed Sun–Mon. Attached to the inn of the same name and serving elegant American cuisine. Excellent chocolate desserts and wine list. Reservations essential.

WILLIAMSBURG

Christiana Campbell's Tavern $$$$ *Waller Street; tel: (888) 965-7254.* Open seasonally; phone for hours. Restored colonial tavern featuring seafood, strolling musicians, costumed servers. Order the Mrs. Campbell's supper sampler. Reservations a must.

Trellis Restaurant $$$–$$$$ *403 Duke of Gloucester Street, Merchants' Square; tel: (757) 229-8610;* www.thetrellis.com. Lunch, dinner daily. Interesting, award winning regional American cooking and fabulous desserts. Reserve well in advance.

A–Z TRAVEL TIPS

A Summary of Practical Information

A

ACCOMMODATIONS

Washington, DC has plenty of hotel rooms, though prices can be a bit steep, especially in summer and spring – prime tourist seasons. Look for off-season, weekend and holiday specials by checking with your travel agent or visiting the hotel's website. Most hotels charge the same for single or double occupants and rates do not include tax, which is 14.5 percent. Most accommodations include private bath and a choice of two single or one king- or queen-sized bed; all offer air conditioning, which is a must in DC. Children can generally stay without charge in their parents' room, though there may be a fee for an additional bed.

Bed-and-breakfasts. Small guesthouses and inns offer rooms from bare bones to luxurious, depending on your budget. Check with the following agencies to book rooms in DC and in nearby Virginia.

Bed and Breakfast Accommodations; tel: (202) 328-3510; or toll free 877 893-3233; www.bedandbreakfastdc.com

Alexandria and Arlington Bed and Breakfast Network; tel: (703) 549-3415; www.aabbn.com

Hostels. International Guest House, 1441 Kennedy Street, NW; tel: (202) 726-5808, www.igh-dc.com

Hostelling International-USA Washington, 1009 11th Street, NW; tel: (202) 737-2333, www.hiwashington.org

AIRPORTS

Dulles International. Most international flights land at Dulles (IAD), about 28 miles (45 km) west of the city in Virginia and about 45 minutes by road, considerably more in rush-hour traffic. Express buses and taxis, operated by the Washington Flyer, offer service between the airport and the city, stopping at several big hotels. Washington Flyer also operates a shuttle-bus service to the West Falls Church Metro station in Virginia. From there you can take the subway into

DC. A Metro extension to the airport is currently under construction and expected to open in 2016. Call (703) 572-6240 for automated flight arrival and departure information or check at www.flydulles.com for schedules and fees.

Baltimore Washington International. Many international flights also land at nearby BWI, just south of Baltimore in Maryland and about 40 miles (64 km) north of Washington. Pick up a taxi or a Super Shuttle van into DC. The trip will take an hour; more in heavy traffic. You can also take a free shuttle bus to the nearby railway station where an Amtrak or MARC train will take you into Washington's Union Station. Metro, DC's public transit system, also runs a bus every 40 minutes between the airport and the Greenbelt Metro Station where you can then take the subway into DC. For information call (410) 859-7111 or check at www.bwiairport.com.

Reagan Washington National. Most domestic flights use National (DCA), as it is more commonly known, just across the Potomac River in Virginia. There's a Metro subway station conveniently located here, and you're only 10 to 20 minutes away by taxi. For information call (703) 417-3500 or check at www.flyreagan.com.

B

BICYCLE RENTAL

Contact the Washington Area Bicyclist Association (WABA) for maps of bike paths; tel: (202) 518-0524; www.waba.org.

Big Wheel Bikes, 1034 33rd Street, NW; tel: (202) 337-0254; www.bigwheelbikes.com

City Bikes, 2501 Champlain Street, NW; tel: (202) 265-1564; www.citybikes.com

Fletcher's Boathouse, 4940 Canal Road, NW; tel: (202) 244-0461; www.fletcherscove.com

Thompson's Boathouse, 2900 Virginia Avenue, NW; tel: (202) 333-9543; www.thompsonboatcenter.com

BUDGETING FOR YOUR TRIP

You can also borrow one of over 3,000 bikes of Capital Bikeshare (www.capitalbikeshare.com) from one of 350 stations in the city and then return it to a station closest to your destination. The first 30 minutes of each trip are free, next minutes incur a fee. To use the bikes you need to join Capital Bikeshare for a day, three days, a month or a year.

BUDGETING FOR YOUR TRIP

To give you an idea of what to expect, here's a list of approximate prices in US dollars:

Airport transfer. From Dulles, about $70 by taxi; about $10 by the Silver Line Express Bus and Metro subway. From BWI, about $80 by taxi; about $30 by train; about $10 by Metro Express Line bus and Metro subway. From National, about $20 by taxi; about $6 by Metro subway.

Bicycle rentals. $15 to $30 per day. Deposit and ID may be required.

Buses. Depending on the route and time of day, $1.75 to $4. Exact change required. (Travel in the city by bus is complicated and best avoided. See Transport.)

Car rental. Prices vary greatly and generally begin at about $25 per day. Weekly rates, membership discounts and weekend deals can lower the daily rate. You'll need a credit card and a valid driver's license. (Driving in DC is not recommended; see Driving.)

Entertainment. Cinema, $12 to $14 (matinees are less); concerts, $20 to $300; theatre $15 to $300; nightclub cover charge $10 to $20, plus drinks $10 to $15.

Hotels. Very expensive, $250 and up; expensive, $200 to $250; moderate, $125 to $200; inexpensive, under $125. Double occupancy; tax not included. Many hotels, however, do have reduced rate packages. Check the hotel websites or phone the hotels directly for details about holiday and weekend specials.

Meals and drinks. Breakfast, $10 and up; lunch, $10 and up; dinner, $15 and up. Carafe of house wine, $15 and up; beer, $4 to $8; spirits, $5 and up; soft drinks, $3 and up; coffee or tea, $3.50 and up.

Metro. To ride Metrorail you need a SmarTrip card, paper farecard or pass. The city's subway (underground) fares vary depending on the traveled distance, the time of day and the type of card used by the passenger. Fares range between $1.75 and $5.90 per one ride. One-, seven- and 28-day SmarTrip passes are available.

Taxis. Fare is based on a meter system. Minimum taxi fare is $3.25, the mileage charge is $0.27 per 1/8 mile. There is also a charge of $1.00 per each additional passenger. Luggage is 50 cents per piece.

C

CAR RENTAL

You can rent cars from one of several national companies with desks at the airports and around the city. Charges vary widely, but there's plenty of competition and choice, so shop around. There can also be a price advantage in reserving well in advance of your arrival. Rates add up quickly when extras such as collision insurance are tacked on, so check your existing coverage to see if it extends to a rental. Automatic transmission and air-conditioning are the norm. You'll need a valid driver's license and you may be asked for your passport. Some companies require an International Driving Permit.

Unless you're planning an out-of-town excursion, you're unlikely to need a car in DC. Traffic is heavy, parking is scarce and expensive, and the streets are tricky to navigate. Instead, use the Metro (the city's subway system), hop on one of the sightseeing buses, or see the city on foot (see Guides and Tours).

CHILDREN

The National Air and Space Museum, the Washington Monument, and the National Zoo are top destinations for children. The National Museum of Natural History features plenty of dinosaurs, along with the impressive Insect Zoo. Ford's Theatre, where Lincoln was shot, and the Bureau of Engraving and Printing, where dollars are printed, are also perennial favorites. The John F. Kennedy Center for the Performing Arts regularly presents children's programs

CLIMATE AND CLOTHING

Climate. Spring, from early April to mid-June, is usually delightful. September and October can be very pleasant. The summer months, however, are hot and humid, and the winters unpredictable.

The following chart gives average daily maximum and minimum temperatures in Washington, DC:

F°	J	F	M	A	M	J	J	A	S	O	N	D
Max	42	44	53	64	75	83	87	84	78	67	55	45
Min	27	28	35	44	54	63	68	66	59	48	38	29
C°	J	F	M	A	M	J	J	A	S	O	N	D
Max	6	7	12	18	24	28	31	29	26	19	13	7
Min	-3	-2	2	7	12	17	20	19	15	9	3	-2

Clothing. Because many people who come to Washington are here for business, the city has a more formal tone than many US cities. More exclusive restaurants require jackets and ties for men, and for women skimpy outfits won't do. Still, casual attire is perfectly acceptable so long as it's tasteful.

Summer's heat can be brutal, so be prepared with lighter weight clothing, but pack a sweater or jacket for the air-conditioned indoors. You'll need a jacket for spring and autumn and if you're visiting in winter be prepared for snow, though it's not guaranteed.

COMMUNICATIONS

Mail. Post offices are open between 9am and 5pm, Monday through Friday, and 9am to noon on Saturday. You can buy stamps from machines in some stores, at the airports and at hotels. The main post office is at L'Enfant Plaza. Other major offices include: Union Station; 1800 M Street, NW; 1200 Pennsylvania Avenue, NW; and 3050 K Street in Georgetown.

Telephone. All telephone numbers in DC, Virginia and Maryland are 10-digit, beginning with the prefix, or area code. These are: DC 202, Virginia 703, and Maryland 301. All calls within these three area codes are local. For directory information, dial the area code and 555-1212, or simply 411. To make any long-distance or toll-free call, first dial 1, then the 10-digit number. Toll-free numbers begin with 800, 844, 855, 866, 877 or 888.

Payphones will accept most calling cards but their number has considerably declined over the last years. The cost of a local call from a pay phone is 50 cents. If you use your cell or mobile phone, bear in mind that calls to local DC numbers may register as long distance.

Hotel charges for making phone calls from your room may be steep. It will probably be considerably cheaper to use a payphone or arm yourself with a pre-paid phonecard.

CRIME AND THEFT

Expect to pass through a metal detector and have your bag searched at all government buildings and tourist attractions. Since September 11, 2001, security all across the city has been heightened and it is taken very seriously. Don't be tempted to joke about it with a security officer, as you may find yourself arrested. Leave your aerosol cans, Swiss Army knives, pepper spray and anything else that might be considered suspect at home or at the hotel, otherwise they will be confiscated.

Those sections of the city of most interest to visitors are generally safe. Nevertheless drug and gang-related violence are a problem in DC, which has one of the country's highest murder rates. Avoid side streets and poorly lit areas after dark. Most crimes are opportunistic, so avoid making yourself a potential victim.

Beware of pickpockets. Keep your handbag securely fastened. Keep your wallet in an inside, never a back, pocket. Know where you're going, how to get there and, most importantly, how to get back. Serious crime on the Metro is rare, though there have been incidents outside Metro stations. Lock your hotel room door and store your valuables, including cash travelers checks, airline tickets, and jewelry, in the hotel safe. Carry only what you will be needing from day to day.

If you are robbed, don't put up a fight. Call the police (911, from any phone) afterward and obtain a copy of the police report to file with your insurance claim. Report stolen traveler's checks and credit cards promptly.

D

DISABLED ACCESS

The Americans with Disabilities Act stipulates that all public places, including museums and other attractions, should be accessible to wheelchair users. Washington is one of the most disabled accessible cities in the world. Most buildings have ramps, elevators, widened doorways and specially marked entrances. Sidewalk curbs all have cuts in them to make it easier to use for wheelchairs, strollers, and bicycles across the city streets.

Public restrooms, including those in restaurants, all have stalls specifically designed for the disabled. Most office buildings, retail stores, and even tour buses and the Metro system can accommodate visitors with disabilities wherever possible.

The best source of information for accessibility and help in the city for people with other types of disability is the Destination DC site·
www.washington.org/DC-information/washington-dc-disability-information

DRIVING

Driving is unnecessary in DC where so much is accessible on foot or by Metro, the city's inexpensive and convenient subway system. But if you must drive, keep to the right and wear your seat belt, which is mandatory. DC's bewildering system of roads, roundabouts, and highways are usually clogged with traffic made worse during morning and evening rush hours. To accommodate rush hour, many traffic lanes reverse direction.

Parking is expensive ($20 a day or more), when you can find it, and gas (petrol), stations are few in the city itself. Added to DC's traffic woes are all the diplomats whose special status means that they are immune from obeying many of the local traffic laws. Get into an accident with one of them and you're on your own.

E

ELECTRIC CURRENT

110-volt 60-cycle A.C. is standard throughout the US. Plugs are the flat, two-pronged (and some three-pronged) variety. Overseas visitors will need a transformer and adapter plug for travel appliances.

EMBASSIES

Just about every country is represented in Washington, DC. Embassies are all located in the northwest of the city, mostly along or near Massachusetts Avenue.

Australia: 1601 Massachusetts Avenue, NW, Washington, DC 20036; tel: (202) 797-3000; www.usa.embassy.gov.au

Canada: 501 Pennsylvania Avenue, NW, Washington, DC 20001; tel: (202) 682-1740; www.can-am.gc.ca/washington

Ireland: 2234 Massachusetts Avenue, NW, Washington, DC 20008; tel: (202) 462-3939; www.dfa.ie/irish-embassy/USA

New Zealand: 37 Observatory Circle, NW, Washington, DC 20008; tel: (202) 328-4800; www.nzembassy.com/usa-washington

South Africa: 3051 Massachusetts Avenue, NW, Washington, DC 20008; tel: (202) 232-4400; www.saembassy.org

United Kingdom: 3100 Massachusetts Avenue, NW, Washington, DC 20008; tel: (202) 588-6500; www.gov.uk/government/world/usa

EMERGENCIES

Dial 911 from any phone and tell the dispatcher the nature of the emergency to summon police, fire or ambulance.

For non-emergencies phone the DC police at (202) 727-9099 or the US Capitol Police at (202) 228-2800.

For travel-related difficulties, contact Travelers' Aid at Union Station (tel: 202-371-1937; http://dc.travelersaid.org), where there's a manned booth Monday through Sat from 9:30am until 5.30pm and on Sunday from 12.30 to 5.30pm. There are also booths at Dulles and Reagan Washington National airports.

G

GAY AND LESBIAN TRAVELERS

The CD Center for the LGBT Community, 2000 14th Street, NW, tel: (202) 682-2245, www.thedccenter.org/. Has all kinds of information about LGBT life in Washington DC. Copies of The Washington Blade newspaper (www.washingtonblade.com), a comprehensive LGBT news source, are available at numerous spots throughout the city and its electronic version may be viewed online. Some of the more popular, long-standing gay clubs in Washington include: DC Eagle, 3701 Benning Road, NE; www.dceagle.com; JR's, 1519 17th Street, NW; tel: (202) 328-0090; www.jrsbar-dc.com and Town Danceboutique, 2009 8th Street, NW; tel: (202) 234-TOWN; www.towndc.com.

GUIDES AND TOURS

To make the most of your visit, put yourself in the hands of one of the city's experienced tour operators such as DC Tours (tel: 212 852-4822; www.dctours.us) who run all kinds of tours including a one- or two-day tour which loops between the various attractions and allows you to get off and then reboard at any stop. Old Town Trolley Tours (tel: 855 629-8777; www.historictours.com) offers similar tours in buses that look like tramcars. Gray Line Tours (tel: 202 779-9894; www.grayline

dc.com) operates from Union Station. Sign on for a moonlight tour to see the monuments when they look their most dramatic.

Water cruises on the Potomac offer a different vantage. Spirit Cruises (tel: 866 404-8439; www.spiritcruises.com/washington-dc) sail from the DC waterfront at 6th and Water streets, SW, for George Washington's Mount Vernon plantation, south of Washington, and on the opposite shore in Virginia. The Potomac Riverboat Company (tel: 703 548-9000; www.potomacriverboatco.com) also cruises to Mount Vernon, and offers excursions between Georgetown and Alexandria, in Virginia, where you can shop and dine.

H

HEALTH AND MEDICAL CARE

Free medical service is not available in the US, and without insurance a visit to a doctor or a hospital can be expensive. Arrange through your own insurance provider, or buy travel insurance with a medical provision before you leave home.

Cost aside, there are several excellent hospitals in the city. They operate a doctor referral system, but if you are unable to wait for an appointment go immediately to the Emergency Room (ER):

Children's National Medical Center, 111 Michigan Avenue, NW; tel: (202) 476-5000; www.childrensnational.org

George Washington University Hospital, 901 23rd Street, NW; tel: (202) 715-4000; www.gwhospital.com

Howard University Hospital, 2041 Georgia Avenue, NW; tel: (202) 865-6100; www.huhealthcare.com

MedStar Georgetown University Hospital, 3800 Reservoir Road, NW; tel: (202) 444-2000; www.medstargeorgetown.org

MedStar Washington Hospital Center, 110 Irving Street, NW; tel: (202) 877-7000; www.medstarwashington.org

You can also dial 911 from any phone or cell phone (mobile) to summon an ambulance.

Pharmacies. The largest pharmacy, or drug store as it's known, is CVS which has branches throughout the city. The CVS at 1199 Vermont Avenue, NW (tel: 202-628-0720) is open 24 hours as is the one at 4555 Wisconsin Avenue, NW (tel: 202-537-1587). Most pharmacies are well stocked with over-the-counter remedies, though you'll need a doctor's prescription for any narcotic or otherwise controlled substance.

The names of some prescription drugs can differ from those in other countries so it's advisable to ask your doctor or pharmacist what the American name is for your prescription medicine, in case of an emergency. The name for paracetamol in the US is acetaminophen with a main brand name of Tylenol.

HITCHHIKING

Hitchhiking is not advisable and usually dangerous, because of traffic flow and volume and issues of personal safety.

INTERNET

You'll have little trouble finding internet access in the city. You can connect at most hotels and many public buildings, including the public library. The main library, the Martin Luther King, Jr. Public Library, is at 9th and G Streets, NW (tel: 202-727-1111). All the library branches offer internet connections as well, including West End, 1101 24th Street, NW at L Street (tel: 202-724-8707), and Georgetown, 3260 R Street, NW (tel: 202-282-0220).

Almost every bookstore also offers internet access. These include Barnes and Noble (555 12th Street, NW; tel: 202-347-0176; www.barnesandnoble.com), Kramerbooks and Afterwords Cafe (1517 Connecticut Avenue, NW; tel: 202-387-1400; www.kramers.com), and Politics and Prose (5015 Connecticut Avenue, NW, tel: 202-364-1919; www.politics-prose.com)

There are also several popular cafes where you can enjoy a light meal while you access the net:

Cosi, 1333 H Street, NW (and many more locations); tel: (202) 289-5888; www.getcosi.com

Starbucks, 1301 Pennsylvania Avenue, NW; tel: (202) 737-7378; also at 700 14th Street, NW; tel: (202) 783-3048; and 1730 Pennsylvania Avenue, NW; tel: (202) 393-1811; www.starbucks.com

Tryst Coffeehouse Bar & Lounge, 2459 18th Street, NW; tel: (202) 232-5500; www.trystdc.com

L

LANGUAGE

US British

admission entry fee
bathroom toilet
bill banknote
check bill (restaurant)
collect call reverse-charge call
comfort station public lavatory
detour diversion
diaper nappy
divided highway dual carriageway
elevator lift
faucet tap
first floor ground floor
gas (gasoline) petrol
general delivery poste restante

line queue
liquor spirits
mail post
outlet socket
pants trousers
restroom public convenience
round-trip ticket return ticket
second floor first floor
stand in line queue up
straight neat (drink)
subway underground
truck lorry
trunk boot (car)
underpass subway

LAUNDRY AND DRY-CLEANING

Many hotels offer a same-day service, and some are even equipped with washers and dryers that guests can use. Several dry cleaners, which are listed in the Yellow Pages of the phone directory, offer a quick turnaround service.

LIQUOR (ALCOHOL) REGULATIONS

The minimum age for buying and consuming alcohol is 21 all over the US. If you look younger than 30, be prepared to show photo identification that proves your age. Most restaurants serve wine by the glass or bottle as well as beer and mixed drinks. Restaurants and nightclubs where drinks are served are often very strict about following the law since an infraction can result in fines and closing. Most grocery and convenience stores carry beer and wine. Spirits are available in liquor stores.

LOST PROPERTY

Most museums, hotels, taxi and tour bus services, and restaurants have a lost-and-found. To check with Metro's lost-and-found, call (202) 962-1195.

M

MAPS AND STREET NAMES

For maps of the city, contact Destination DC, 901 7th Street, NW; tel. (202) 789-7000; www.washington.org.

The city is laid out in quadrants: Northwest, Northeast, Southwest and Southeast. Each quadrant runs in a compass direction from the US Capitol. Numbered streets run north to south; lettered streets run east to west. There are no J, X, Y, or Z streets, and I Street is sometimes written "Eye" for clarity. It's important to include the quadrant designation – NW, NE, SW, SE – with all street addresses, since the same numbers and letters may appear in each quadrant.

Avenues are named for each of the states and cut diagonally across the grid, intersecting at various circles and squares. It sounds sensible enough, but it can be devilishly difficult for newcomers to navigate this warren of roads, which are not always well-marked and sometimes reach a dead-end only to pick up again on the other side of a physical obstacle. Keep a map handy.

MONEY MATTERS

Currency. The dollar ($) is divided into 100 cents (¢).

Coins: 1¢ (penny), 5¢ (nickel), 10¢ (dime), 25¢ (quarter), 50¢ (half dollar), and $1.

Banknotes (bills): $1, $2 (uncommon), $5, $10, $20, $50, and $100. Larger denominations ($500, $1,000) are not in general circulation. Most denominations are the same size and the same black-and-green color, so be sure to check each one before paying. New editions of the $5, $10, $20, $50, and $100 bills differ from the older versions, with larger portraits on the front and additional coloring. These new bills are in circulation along with the older versions of the same denominations.

It's worth carrying a supply of dimes, quarters, and $1 notes for tips, telephone calls, and small purchases.

For currency restrictions, see Customs and Entry Formalities.

Banks and currency exchange. Banking hours vary, but are typically from 8:30 or 9am to 3pm Monday through Friday. A few banks are open on Saturday mornings. Smaller branches will not change foreign cash. There are exchanges at the airports and in main hotels, but their rates are generally poorer.

ATMs (automated teller machines, or cashpoints) can be found in many stores and hotel lobbies, as well as on the street, but the former usually charge a hefty service fee.

Credit and charge cards. "Plastic" money plays an even greater role in the US than in Europe: it's a way of life. The major cards (American Express, Diners Club, MasterCard/Access/Eurocard, Visa and associates, and Discover) are accepted almost everywhere. When paying, you'll often be asked "cash or charge?"

Traveler's checks. You'll find traveler's checks in US dollars drawn on American banks much easier to use, and more often accepted as cash. Only exchange small amounts at a time, keeping the balance in a hotel safe if possible. Keep a record of the serial numbers in a separate place from the checks in case of loss or theft.

Sales taxes. All meals, hotel rooms and most purchases, except those you make in many of the museum shops, are assessed a sales tax. In DC, the sales tax on goods is 6.75 percent; on restaurant meals it's 10 percent; for a hotel room the tax is 14.5 percent. Virginia and Maryland have similar sales taxes.

N

NEWSPAPERS AND MAGAZINES

The Washington Post and The Washington Times are dailies covering the political scene, national and local news, and events. The Friday "Weekend" section of the Washington Post includes a useful entertainment guide.

International news is better covered in The New York Times and The Wall Street Journal. These, and the London Financial Times, printed in the US, are sold at newsstands and vending machines.

Look for the free weekly Washington City Paper (www.washingtoncitypaper.com) for events, entertainment, and inside stories. The free monthly magazine Where (www.wheretraveler.com) is distributed through hotels, and the lively Washingtonian (www.washingtonian.com) carries restaurant reviews and stories about the capital.

Only a few newsstands sell a large selection of foreign papers.

O

OPENING HOURS

Most museums are open every day except Christmas Day. The Smithsonian museums are open from 10am to 5:30pm. Some of the smaller museums, historic houses, and galleries are closed on Mondays. Shopping hours are generally from 10am to 5pm or 6pm, Monday through Saturday, with Sunday hours starting at noon. Some restaurants close on Sundays or Mondays.

P

PHOTOGRAPHY AND VIDEO

All popular brands of film and camera equipment are available. Check ProPhoto (2000 Pennsylvania Avenue, NW) or District Camera and Imaging (1735 Connecticut Avenue, NW). Same-day print service is available at many pharmacies, grocery stores, and at Ritz Photo, a local chain with many branches. (Check the phone book in your hotel.) If you're using film and not digital, remember to avoid exposing film to airport x-ray machines; ask for hand inspection.

POLICE

For emergencies, dial 911 from any phone. For non-emergencies, phone the DC police at (202) 727-9099 (www.mpdc.dc.gov) or the US Capitol Police at (202) 228-2800 (www.uscapitolpolice.gov). DC is also patrolled by the National Park Police whose officers you'll see around the Mall and at many of the monuments, and the Metro Police, who serve the city's transit system. It is also headquarters to the FBI, the Secret Service and the CIA. Never hesitate to approach an officer from any branch for help of any kind.

PUBLIC (LEGAL) HOLIDAYS

In most states, the following days are public holidays. If a holiday falls on a Sunday, banks and many stores close on the following day. Some Thursday holidays stretch into a long weekend.

1 January *New Year's Day*
Third Monday in January *Martin Luther King Day*
12 February *Lincoln's Birthday*
Third Monday in February *Washington's Birthday*
Last Monday in May *Memorial Day*
4 July *Independence Day*
First Monday in September *Labor Day*
Second Monday in October *Columbus Day*

11 November *Veterans' Day*
Fourth Thursday in November *Thanksgiving Day*
25 December *Christmas Day*

R

RADIO AND TELEVISION

Washington has three network broadcast stations: NBC (WRC-TV), ABC (WJLA-TV) and CBS (WUSA-TV). Cable television also carries CNN, the Discovery Channels, sports, films, children's programming and more. National Public Radio offers excellent news and public affairs programming all through the day.

RELIGIOUS SERVICES

Every possible denomination is represented in Washington. Check the Yellow Pages of the phone book or with your hotel's concierge.

Some of the oldest and largest congregations occupying some of the grandest spaces include: Basilica of the National Shrine of the Immaculate Conception (Roman Catholic), Michigan Avenue and 4th Street, NE; tel: (202) 526-8300; www.nationalshrine.com; Washington National Cathedral (Episcopal) 3001 Wisconsin Avenue, NW; tel: (202) 537-6200; www.cathedral.org; Temple Sinai, 3100 Military Road, NW; tel: (202) 363-6394; www.templesinaidc.org; Islamic Center, 2551 Massachusetts Avenue, NW; tel: (202) 332-8343; www.theislamiccenter.com.

S

SMOKING

Though cigarettes, cigars and tobacco are widely available in grocery and convenience stores, newsstands, and through vending machines, smoking is banned in most public buildings and restaurants. Tobacco products are also expensive.

TIMES AND DATES

Washington, DC is in the US Eastern Standard Time Zone, which is five hours behind GMT The clock is advanced by one hour to Daylight Savings Time (GMT minus 4 hours) between the first Sunday in April and the last Sunday in October, dates that are not quite synchronized with European countries. The following chart shows the time in various cities in summer when it is noon in Washington.

L.A.	Washington, DC	London	Sydney
9am	noon	5pm	2am
Sunday	Sunday	Sunday	Monday

Dates in the US are written in the order month/day/year; for example, 9/6/15 means 6 September 2015.

TIPPING

Tipping is expected and 20 percent in restaurants and bars is the norm. Even in fast-food and self-serve restaurants it's customary to leave a dollar. Credit card receipts are left "open" so that you may fill in the tip before signing. Cash is also acceptable. Cinema and theater ushers are not tipped, but doormen, cloakroom attendants, lavatory attendants, and anyone else who has rendered a service should be tipped. Here are some suggested guidelines:

Hotel porters and airport skycaps: no less than $2 per bag
Hotel maids: 10 percent of the daily room rate for each day
Taxi drivers: 10 to 15 percent
Hairdressers and barber: 15-20 percent

TOILETS

These are plentiful, usually found off the lobbies of the larger hotels, in shopping malls and larger stores, and within every museum, especially the museums on the Mall where they're clean and spacious. Memorials and outdoor sites, however, do not have facilities. Keep this in mind when you're planning to tour the monuments on the Mall.

TOURIST INFORMATION OFFICES

You'll find a comprehensive collection of brochures and maps, plus friendly assistance at Destination DC, 901 7th Street, 4th Floor, NW, Washington, DC 20001-3719; tel: (202) 789-7000; www.washington.org.

For information about the Smithsonian, call (202) 633-1000 or visit www.si.edu. For the National Gallery of Art, which is on the Mall but not part of the Smithsonian, call (202) 737-4215, or visit www.nga.gov. For information about the White House, contact the White House Visitor Center, 1450 Pennsylvania Avenue, NW; tel: (202) 208-1631, www.whitehouse.gov; www.nps.gov/whho.

For travel-related difficulty, contact Travelers' Aid at Union Station (tel: 202-371-1937; http://dc.travelersaid.org), where there's a manned booth Monday through Sat from 9:30am until 5.30pm and on Sunday from 12.30 to 5.30pm. There are also booths at Dulles and Reagan Washington National Airports.

TRANSPORT

WMATA (Washington Metropolitan Area Transit Authority) runs a combined rail (Metrorail) and road (Metrobus) network. Maps are available from some Metro stations and from WMATA, 600 5th Street, NW; Telephone inquiries: (202) 637-7000; www.wmata.com).

Metrorail rapid transit train system is a revelation to anyone who's used to London's cramped underground or New York's subway. This one is more like Moscow's, without the art. With huge coffered vaults modeled on Rome's Pantheon, the longest escalators in the world, and walls separated from platforms by deep dry moats so they can't be reached by would-be graffiti artists, it's like a set for a science fiction film. The pillar-less design makes for security: there's no place to hide from surveillance cameras. Cleanliness is remarkable – even the carpets (yes, carpets) are vacuumed daily. The cost has reached 11 figures and some lines are still unbuilt: cynics calculate that everyone in DC could have been given a nice car for the money.

Except for Georgetown, nearly everywhere you are likely to visit is within 10 minutes' walk of a Metrorail station. They're marked by discreet (often hard to spot) brown posts capped by an "M." Maps, information, and batteries of ticket machines stand at the bottom end of the escalators. To ride Metrorail you need a SmarTrip card, paper farecard or pass. The machines take coins and banknotes; change is in coins. Select the card value you want. At the end of each trip, the exit gate will stamp the remaining value on it. You can exchange it when you want by feeding it, and more money, into a machine.

Lines are denoted by colors: red, orange, silver, green, blue and yellow. Trains and platform indicators bear the name of the end-of-the-line destination. The system closes at midnight.

You can buy a one-day Metrorail SmarTrip pass for $14.50 which simplifies the sometimes complicated farecard system, and allows you to make unlimited trips on Metrorail on one day. There are also 7-day and 28-day SmarTrip passes.

Buses. The Metrobus system is complex. Even the locals don't know all about it. Many bus lines run only in rush hours. Ask your hotel concierge and other travelers at the bus stop to find which line you want. Check with the driver as you get on to ensure you are going the right way. The exact fare is needed, as you put it into a box when you board and drivers don't carry change (regular fare is $1.75 and express fare is $4). Ask for a "transfer" (free) if you are likely to want to continue the journey in the same general direction on another bus. You cannot get a free transfer to a Metro train.

There is no Metrorail service into Georgetown, but there is a bus that runs every 10 minutes between the nearest Metro station, Foggy Bottom, and Georgetown along popular M Street.

Taxis. There are plenty of cabs, except when it rains. They can be hailed as they pass by, picked up at countless waiting points, or called by telephone (the companies are listed in the Yellow Pages under Taxicabs). City-based cabs have meters: Minimum taxi fare is $3.25, the mileage charge is $0.27 per 1/8 mile. There is also a charge of $1.00 per each additional passenger. Luggage is 50 cents per piece. In less busy streets and rush hours, drivers will stop to pick up extra passengers, but there's no saving on the fare for such a shared ride. Tipping is normal, rounding up the fare by 10–15 per cent. Don't expect all taxi drivers to know the city, and especially the suburbs, very well.

TRAVELING TO WASHINGTON, DC

Because of the complexity and variability of the many fares available, you need to speak to an informed travel agent well before your date of travel.

By Air

International flights. Most major airlines operate flights to Washington, DC, which is served by three airports (see Airports).

Apart from standard first class, business/club, and economy fares, main types of fare available are: APEX (book 21 days prior to departure for stays of 7 days to 6 months, no stopovers); Special Economy (book any time, offers plenty of flexibility); Standby (only on the day of travel, generally restricted to summer). Off-season reduced fares and many package deals are also available.

For travelers from Europe, it is occasionally less expensive to buy a round-trip (return) ticket to New York and to continue to Washington, DC by road, rail, or with a domestic airline. However, airline fares have been fluctuating so much recently, it is probably best to consult a travel agent or the internet.

Domestic flights. There is daily service between Washington, DC and at least one city in every state of the Union, as well as larger Canadian cities. Hourly shuttles operate between Washington, DC and New York or Boston on a first-come, first-served basis. Major destinations are linked with Washington, DC by non-stop flights: the airlines' hub systems necessitate a change of plane before you reach most smaller and more distant places.

Baggage. You are allowed to check two pieces of baggage of normal size on scheduled transatlantic flights and flights within the United States and Canada. On other international flights the allowance will vary between 44 pounds (20 kg) and 88 pounds (40 kg), depending on what class you are traveling.

In addition to checked baggage, one piece of hand luggage that fits easily under the aircraft seat or in the overhead lockers may be carried on board. Check size and weight limits with your travel agent or airline when booking your ticket (which will also show the weight allowance).

It is advisable to insure all luggage for the duration of your trip, possibly as part of a travel insurance package; talk to your travel agent.

By Bus

If you're not particular about your traveling companions and are willing to put up with an unreliable service and less than spotless accommodations, travel by bus is an inexpensive alternative. For fares and scheduling, contact: Greyhound Bus Lines, 50 Massachusetts Avenue, NE; tel: (202) 269-5141, 1-800-231-2222 (toll free); www.greyhound.com.

By Rail

Amtrak trains link Union Station with the main cities of the northeast corridor and some in the South. Amtrak's *Acela Express* is 2 hours and 45 minutes service that operates between Washington, DC and New York City.

Discount tickets and special package tours are available. If you're planning to travel extensively by train, consider buying regional passes. For information, call 1-800-USA-RAIL. For foreigners, there's the USA Railpass, on sale abroad, and at major railway stations in the US.

V

VISAS AND ENTRY REQUIREMENTS

For entry into the US you'll need a visa, a passport, the address of where you'll be staying, as well as evidence of your intent to leave the US. Citizens of some countries, including the UK, Australia, New Zealand and Ireland, can visit under the guidelines of the Visa Waiver Program (Canadian citizens don't require a visa to enter the U.S.). You will be finger-printed and photographed.

At customs your bags will be inspected. You may bring up to $10,000 into the US, as many as 200 cigarettes, gifts valued at less than $400, and only such prescription drugs as you'll need during your stay. Customs requirements are often changed, so it's advisable to double check before you go at www.travel.state.gov/content/visas/en.html or www.cbp.gov/travel.

W

WEBSITES

The following are some useful websites.

www.washington.org is an official tourism site of Washington DC, provides information from Destination DC

www.washingtonpost.com The Washington Post's website

www.si.edu covers all the Smithsonian Institution's museums

www.nga.gov gives the lowdown on what's on at the National Gallery of Art

www.wmata.com is the site of the Washington Metropolitan Area Transit Authority (Metro)

WEIGHTS AND MEASURES

Milk and fruit juice can be bought by the quart or half-gallon, but wine and spirits come in liter bottles. Food products usually have the weight marked in ounces and pounds, as well as in grams.

RECOMMENDED HOTELS

The price categories given below are relative; there is no definable high or low season for travel to Washington, DC. In general, count on hotel prices being higher when cherry blossoms are in bloom (late March through early April) and when Congress is in session (mid-September through Thanksgiving and mid-January through June). Also, rates are significantly higher during the week. Contact the hotel directly to see if you can beat their published price; many of the places listed below offer special packages for families, couples, seniors, groups, and government employees that include breakfast and other extras.

Virtually every hotel mentioned here offers a standard roster of amenities: cable TV, ironing boards and irons, hair dryers, in-room coffeemakers and safes. Toll-free numbers work in the US only.

For still more choices, and to make online reservations, visit www. washingtondchotels.com.

Unless otherwise noted, the hotels listed accept major credit cards (American Express, MasterCard, Visa).

$$$$	Above $250
$$$	$200–250
$$	$125–200
$	Below $125

CAPITOL HILL AND UNION STATION

Capitol Hill Hotel $$ *200 C Street, SE; tel: (202) 543-6000;* www. capitolhillhotel-dc.com. These converted apartment houses on a residential street across from the Library of Congress, are well suited for families (continental breakfast included; children under 18 stay free). The one-bedroom accommodations are roomy, with living/dining areas as well as either full kitchens or kitchenettes (there's a nearby market where you can buy provisions). Décor is pleasant, fitted out with mahogany furniture. 153 suites. Metro: Capitol South.

Capital Hilton $$$–$$$$ *16th Street, between K and L streets. NW;* tel: (202) 393-1000; www.hilton.com. An easy walk to the White House, many of the monuments, and shopping, with spacious rooms. Catch shuttle buses to National and Dulles airports next door. Children stay free. 544 rooms. Metro: Farragut West, Farragut North, or McPherson Square.

Crowne Plaza The Hamilton $$ *14th and K streets. NW; tel: (202)* 682-0111; www.ihg.com. A warm, pleasant hotel overlooking Franklin Square. The Beaux-Arts lobby is welcoming, with fresh flowers and plush upholstered furniture. Rooms are decorated in subtle earth tones and floral prints. Some rooms have a view of the Washington Monument. 318 rooms. Metro: McPherson Square.

Grand Hyatt Washington $$$–$$$$ *1000 H Street, NW; tel: (202)* 582-1234; www.grandwashington.hyatt.com. The emphasis here is on "grand," with a glassed-in lobby buzzing with activity. Rooms are all luxury with marble baths. Fitness center and four dining rooms. 897 rooms. Metro: Center.

Hay Adams $$$$ *16th and H streets. NW; tel: (202) 638-6600, (800)* 553-6807; www.hayadams.com. Caters to the rich and powerful. Public areas are outfitted with antique furnishings; many guest rooms have silk bedspreads and fine art. For a straight-on view of the White House (one block away), ask for a room facing H Street. 145 rooms. Metro: Farragut West or McPherson Square.

Hotel Monaco $$$$ *700 F Street, NW; tel: (202) 628-7177, (800) 649-* 1202; www.monaco-dc.com. Once a crumbling ruin, the city's old post office has been fully restored to its former marble glory and converted into a luxury hotel. An attentive staff, impressive public art, and extras such as 300-count Frette cotton sheets are hallmarks. Dog-friendly, this hotel even provides a walking service. Metro: Metro Center.

The Jefferson $$$$ *1200 16th Street, NW; tel: (202) 448-2300, (877)* 313-9749; www.jeffersondc.com. A small, ultra-luxurious boutique hotel: Guest rooms are quietly elegant; many boast canopy beds and antique bookcases filled with rare books. Excellent dining room; serves afternoon tea. 95 rooms. Metro: Farragut North.

Mayflower Hotel $$$$ *1127 Connecticut Avenue, NW; tel: (202) 347-3000, 1-(800) 228-7697;* www.marriott.com. Long the venue for presidential inaugural balls (and the one-time home of fdr), this 10-story hotel is on the National Register of Historic Places. The restaurant and bar are gathering spots for politicos. 657 rooms. Metro: Farragut North.

Morrison-Clark Inn $$ *Massachusetts Avenue, at 11th Street, NW; tel: (202) 898-1200, 1-(800) 332-7898;* www.morrisonclark.com. Victorian touches pop up in the common rooms and extend to the guest rooms – lace curtains, carved armoires, and 19th-century engravings. Rates include continental breakfast. Ask about special rates. Children under 12 stay free. The hotel has a total of 114 rooms. Metro: Metro Center.

St Regis Washington $$$$ *923 16th Street, NW; tel: (202) 638-2626;* www.stregiswashingtondc.com. Rooms are luxurious, and the hotel reopened in 2008 after a landmark renovation. Just three blocks from the White House, the hotel offers free morning shuttle service anywhere within a 5-mile (8-km) radius. 175 rooms. Metro: Farragut West or McPherson Square.

W Washington DC Hotel $$–$$$ *15th and Pennsylvania Avenue, NW; tel: (202) 661-2400;* www.wwashingtondc.com. The oldest continuously operating hotel in Washington. Rooms have a colonial feel, with traditional furnishings. The top floor terrace/café and restaurant provide marvelous views of the Washington Monument. Order dessert and watch the sunset. 317 rooms. Metro: Metro Center.

Willard Washington D.C. $$$$ *1401 Pennsylvania Avenue, NW; tel: (202) 628-9100, (800) 311-1216;* www.washington.interconti.com. The Willard is a Beaux-Arts gem, a restored national landmark that's long been the choice of statesmen (Abraham Lincoln), literary legends (Charles Dickens), and a host of foreign leaders. Rooms are spacious and elegant, decorated in Federal style. 335 rooms. Metro: Metro Center.

Embassy Suites $$ 1250 22nd Street, NW; tel: (202) 857 3388; www. embassysuites.com This cheerful hotel, built around a nine-story atrium, features two-room suites each with two televisions, fridge, microwave, and dining table. 318 suites.

Four Seasons $$$$ 2800 Pennsylvania Avenue, NW; tel: (202) 342-0444; www.fourseasons.com/washington. This glamorous Georgetown hotel's rooms are understated yet extravagant, with down comforters (duvets), antique framed prints, and plump divans in muted tones. Starlets and regular folks alike get the same friendly, efficient service. Children under 16 stay free. 222 rooms.

Graham Hotel $$ 1075 Thomas Jefferson Street, NW; tel: (202) 337-0900, (855) 341-1292; www.thegrahamgeorgetown.com. Foreign embassy employees and celebrities are frequent guests to this hotel: Offers one- or two-bedroom suites. Rates include continental breakfast and free use of nearby health clubs. 57 suites. Metro: Foggy Bottom.

Holiday Inn Georgetown $–$$ 2101 Wisconsin Avenue, NW; tel: (202) 338-4600, (800) 311-1216, www.holidayinn.com. One of Washington's best-kept secrets. Well-kept rooms decorated in subtle blue-greys Rooms on the fifth to seventh floors have lovely views of the Potomac River and Washington Monument. Just a short jaunt downhill from Georgetown's main street. 284 rooms.

Melrose Hotel $$ 2430 Pennsylvania Avenue, NW; tel: (202) 955-6400; www.melrosehoteldc.com. The multilingual staff attracts an international clientele to this small, quiet hotel located halfway between Georgetown and downtown. Elegant, classic furnishings. Small health club with access to nearby larger facilities. Upgrades and special packages often available. 240 rooms. Metro: Foggy Bottom.

Park Hyatt $$$$ 1201 24th Street, NW; tel: (202) 789-1234; www.park washington.hyatt.com. The Park Hyatt is one block from Rock Creek Park, a quiet spot halfway between downtown attractions and Georgetown's shopping and nightlife. Modern-style furnishings, fitness center, pool, spa. 216 rooms. Metro: Foggy Bottom or Dupont Circle.

Residence Inn Washington $$ *801 New Hampshire Avenue, NW; tel:* *(202) 785-2000;* www.marriott.com. The Residence Inn caters to long-term guests. One-bedroom apartments have living and dining areas and a full kitchen with microwave. Located on a quiet residential block around the corner from Kennedy Center. 103 suites. Metro: Foggy Bottom.

Washington Fairmont $$$$ *2401 M Street, NW; tel: (202) 429-2400;* *1-(866) 540-4505;* www.fairmont.com. Outfitted with a mix of contemporary and antique furnishings and original art. Fitness center and pool. Accepts pets with some stipulations. 415 rooms. Metro: Foggy Bottom.

Watergate Hotel $$$$ *2650 Virginia Avenue, NW; tel: (202) 827-1600;* www.thewatergatehotel.com. This swank legendary hotel next to the Kennedy Center reopened in 2015 after a $125 million renovation, wonderfully blending mid-century modern design with subtle references to the hotel's past (Watergate scandal). Rooftop bar with charming waterfront views. On-site spa. Excellent restaurants and high-end shops, plus the legendary Watergate Pastry nearby. 337 rooms. Metro: Foggy Bottom.

ADAMS MORGAN & DUPONT CIRCLE

Churchill Hotel $$$ *1914 Connecticut Avenue, NW; tel: (202) 797-2000,* *(800) 424-2464;* www.thechurchillhotel.com. This hotel gets a lot of international business; it's close to most of Washington's embassies. Accommodations are roomy, and those on the Connecticut Avenue side have views of downtown. Ask about weekend getaway packages. 173 rooms. Metro: Dupont Circle.

Embassy Inn/Windsor Inn $$ *Embassy Inn: 1627 16th Street, NW; tel:* *(202) 234-7800, 1-(877) 968-9111;* www.embassy-inn-hotel-dc.com; *Windsor Inn: 1842 16th Street, NW tel: (202) 667-0300;* www.windsor-inn-hotel-dc.com. These turn-of-the-century brick twins are converted apartment houses. Scrupulously neat rooms with mini-fridges. Complimentary breakfast and evening sherry. 36 rooms. Metro: Dupont Circle.

Fairfax at Embassy Row $$$ *2100 Massachusetts Avenue, NW; tel: (202) 293-2100; www.starwood.com/westin.* This chic, stately hotel fits in perfectly with the grand mansions along Embassy Row. Rooms are sumptuous with rich brocade fabrics and marble baths. Rooms on higher floors overlook either Embassy Row or Georgetown. Children under 18 stay free. 259 rooms. Metro: Dupont Circle.

Kalorama Guest House $ *2700 Cathedral Avenue, NW; tel: (202) 588-8180; www.kaloramaguesthouse.com.* An inexpensive B&B popular with young people. Quirky and homey – two houses furnished with eclectic antiques. Rates include continental breakfast. 19 rooms (some of them have private baths). Metro: Woodley Park-Zoo.

Tabard $$ *1739 N Street, NW; tel: (202) 785-1277; www.tabardinn.com.* 19th-century townhouse turned inn on a quiet but close-in side street. Great location. Rooms have more character than convenience; some with private baths. The tiny restaurant is a favorite, especially for Sunday brunch. 40 rooms. Metro: Farragut North or Dupont Circle.

Washington Hilton and Towers $$$-$$$$ *1919 Connecticut Avenue, NW; tel: (202) 483-3000; www.hilton.com.* Popular with conventioneers. Standard rooms; those above the fifth floor have panoramic views over the city. Outdoor, heated Olympic-size pool and tennis courts. 1,070 rooms. Metro: Dupont Circle.

BALTIMORE

Admiral Fell Inn $$-$$$ *888 S Broadway; tel: (410) 522-7380; www.admiralfell.com.* This appealing inn has served as both a boardinghouse and a vinegar factory. Now, it's a good getaway spot, some rooms have Jacuzzis and canopied beds. Just one block from Baltimore's harbor, in Fells Point, a neighborhood full of boutiques, restaurants, and bars. 80 rooms.

Royal Sonesta Harbor Court Baltimore $$$ *550 Light Street; tel: (410) 234-0550; www.sonesta.com/baltimore.* A charming brick hotel right on the waterfront. Rooms are decorated with antique reproduction furniture; ask for a room facing the harbor. 200 rooms.

Boar's Head Inn $$ *200 Ednam Drive; tel: (855) 452-2295;* www.boars headinn.com. Run by the University of Virginia, the Boar's Head Inn is a semi-modern facility built around a historic gristmill that houses the inn's tavern and restaurant. Some rooms have fireplaces and views of an adjacent lake. A good jumping-off point for touring Charlottesville, Jefferson's Monticello home, and the region's excellent wineries. 175 rooms.

Keswick Hall $$$–$$$$ *701 Club Drive, Keswick, VA; tel: (434) 979-3440, (888) 778-2565;* www.keswick.com. Keswick succeeds at being an English country inn right in the hometown of the founding father of American independence Thomas Jefferson. Romantic and exclusive, with Laura Ashley-inspired décor. Arnold Palmer was responsible for the golf links. Nearby wineries, the Blue Ridge Mountains, charming Charlottesville, and the University of Virginia, Jefferson's "academical village." 48 rooms.

Clarion Hotel Historic District $–$$ *351 York Street; tel: (757) 229-4100;* www.choicehotels.com. Across the street from Colonial Williamsburg and just a short hop to Busch Gardens and the area's golf courses. Suites come equipped with complete kitchen. Indoor pool on premises. 198 rooms.

Williamsburg Inn $$$$ *136 Francis Street; tel: (757) 220-7978, (888) 965-7254;* www.colonialwilliams *burg.com.* This magnificent hotel looks like an ancestral estate. Foreign leaders and presidents galore have enjoyed the inn's charms. Accommodations are in either the main inn building or one of the adjacent colonial houses and taverns. Tour the Yorktown Battlefield, site of the Revolution's end, plus nearby Jamestown, where the first English settlers landed. The golfing here is top-notch; museums, beaches and other attractions close by. 91 rooms and 14 suites.

INSIGHT ⊙ GUIDES POCKET GUIDE

WASHINGTON, DC

First Edition 2016

Editor: Kate Drynan
Author: Martin Gostelow, Rosanne Scott
Head of Production: Rebeka Davies
Picture Editor: Tom Smyth
Cartography Update: Carte
Update Production: AM Services
Photography Credits: Bigstock 88; Freer Gallery of Art 61; Getty Images 4MC, 4ML, 6ML, 22, 27, 78, 90, 94, 99; iStock 4TL, 5MC, 5M, 8R, 9, 20, 28, 42, 44, 56, 59, 77; Leonard Phillips/Virginia Tourism Corporation 87; Leonardo 46; Nowitz Photography/Apa Publications 4TC, 5T, 5TC, 5MC, 5M, 6MC, 6ML, 7M, 7T, 7M, 8L, 9R, 11, 25, 31, 32, 35, 36, 39, 40, 51, 53, 54, 64, 68, 70, 74, 80, 83, 84, 92, 97, 100, 103, 104; Public domain 13, 14, 16, 19, 73; Shutterstock 7TC, 49; Slipstream 6TL; Smithsonian 63, 67; United States Holocaust Memorial Museum 6TL
Cover Picture: iStock

Distribution

UK: Dorling Kindersley Ltd,
A Penguin Group company, 80 Strand, London, WC2R 0RL; sales@uk.dk.com
United States: Ingram Publisher Services,
1 Ingram Boulevard, PO Box 3006, La Vergne, TN 37086-1986; ips@ingramcontent.com
Australia and New Zealand: Woodslane,

10 Apollo St, Warriewood, NSW 2102, Australia; info@woodslane.com.au
Worldwide: Apa Publications (Singapore) Pte, 7030 Ang Mo Kio Avenue 5, 08-65 Northstar @ AMK, Singapore 569880 apasin@singnet.com.sg

Contact us

Every effort has been made to provide accurate information in this publication, but changes are inevitable. The publisher cannot be responsible for any resulting loss, inconvenience or injury. We would appreciate it if readers would call our attention to any errors or outdated information. We also welcome your suggestions; please contact us at: hello@insightguides.com
www.insightguides.com